The Home Book of
American Cookery

The Home Book of
American Cookery

NINETTE LYON and
BRUCE H. AXLER

FABER AND FABER
3 Queen Square
London

First published in 1973
by Faber and Faber Limited
3 Queen Square London WC1
Printed in Great Britain by
Western Printing Services Ltd Bristol

ISBN 0 571 10136 4

Contents

Contents

MAP OF
The United States
of America

showing states, state capitals, and areas of
principal cuisines

Introduction

The American cuisine today is a mixture of cuisines from the whole world, adapted, transformed and reinvented, but perhaps paradoxically, it *is* uniquely American. It could only exist in America and only in America of the seventies. For the first time in human experience, an entire people is so well fed and so prosperous that their eating has become a cultural phenomenon. Today less than nineteen per cent of a family's disposable income goes on food, which is so cheap, so plentiful and so varied for most Americans that their food choices are virtually independent of the physical need to eat.

Until comparatively recently, many Americans ate like many poor people in Europe. Perhaps they had a little more meat, but generally they ate high carbohydrate foods cooked in the simplest manner.

In the early history of America, near starvation was a way of life, survival the only imperative. People ate what they were obliged to eat or perished. The failure of the Jamestown colony in Virginia was a failure to abandon European values and adapt. The success of the pilgrim colonization of New England was in the fortunate coincidence of conservative Puritan values and a situation that did not allow the least indulgence or luxury.

A number of factors which shape cuisine today have their origin in the nineteenth century. In the middle of the century, immigrants of middle Europe introduced new concepts of nutrition and diet without, at that time, really affecting anyone except a few wealthy city dwellers. Others in the cities and on the farms were unmoved by talk of protective foods and vegetable diets. Not only were they ignorant and suspicious, they were proud.

Later in the nineteenth century, urbanization eroded some of the conservatism present earlier, but not always for the better. Food pretensions replaced asceticism. Instead of buying cheap, wholesome food, the urban poor spent their money, when they had any, on status foods. This use of food to assert one's social position occurs throughout American history. Even in the depression of the thirties, poor whites in the south rejected fish, both plentiful and cheap, as suited for negroes. Today, although few people must sacrifice nutrition for their pretensions, food is still used to assert status. Technological advances in food processing in the nineteenth century allowed food purveyors to cater for these pretensions. Patent bleached flour and white sugar, both prestige foods, rapidly replaced whole grain flours and natural sugars to the everlasting detriment of the lower paid classes.

For most Americans, the supermarket is their kitchen garden and dairy herd. Almost two thousand new products are introduced each year. Customarily, the supermarket has seven departments: meat, produce, dairy, frozen foods, bakery, grocery and non-food department. In the meat department shoppers can choose from packages that are pre-cut, weighed, priced, and wrapped in transparent film. The particular variety offered, how much, which cut, has been carefully researched. Americans seldom find well-marbled beef in supermarkets; research indicates that lean, compact, smaller cuts have more appeal for the consumer. A great deal of beef is cut from light carcasses, because the shopper with a family of four would prefer four small steaks to one large steak. Likewise, beef is not aged to develop flavour. American housewives do not accept beef with an aged look: it must always appear a bright, cherry red.

Introduction

For the most part, offals, even the most choice ones, go begging. Ironically, a pair of veal kidneys in a specialty butcher's shop catering to 'sophisticated' clients may cost a dollar and a half, while in a neighbourhood supermarket they are incidental products of other butchering and may cost thirty-five cents. Liver, widely touted by the nutritionists, is the only exception. Its price is relatively consistent.

Little game is sold in supermarkets, even in areas such as Wyoming, where game represents a third of the meat consumption. If anything is carried, it is Cornish game hen, a crossbreed chicken more mild than the mildest squab.

Mutton is not available. Sheep are butchered for lamb, primarily for their rib and loin chops, and, to a lesser extent, for their legs. Other parts, especially the cartilaginous portion with which American cooks cannot deal, are great bargains. Although spareribs, ham, pork chops and belly bacon have a wide sale, the emphasis throughout most of the United States is on beef.

The average weight of poultry sold in the States is three pounds; few Americans have ever seen a pullet or stewing hen. Very little distinction is drawn among poultry brands or varieties. Buy a broiler anywhere in the United States and you can expect an immaculate little bird of a pound and a half or two pounds, eight weeks old, with fine-grained, yellowish-white skin, a full, plump breast, absolutely no pin feathers, and no viscera except for a small packet containing the giblets, heart and liver. Turkeys remain a seasonal food, in greatest supply at Christmas and Thanksgiving, although frozen birds, boned turkey loaves, and turkey rolls are available year-round.

More fish is canned, frozen and cured than is sold fresh. Fresh fish is sold primarily in speciality stores. With the exception of lobster and shrimp, fish is not favoured by most inland Americans, perhaps because they have never seen any fresh fish. Pollution has devastated the once plentiful freshwater supplies. Test surveys have found that Mid-westerners actually do have an aversion to fresh fish, and prefer the frozen product.

Few vegetables in America are seasonal; the country is so vast and so varied that there is a year-round growing season for most products. While the source of the supply may vary geographically, the consumer is hardly affected. Much fruit is shipped by air. In fact, within the next few years, even live cattle are expected to be flown to market. Some fruits and vegetables are chilled in the field and stored in controlled atmospheres to ensure good produce in the market months after harvesting.

Although the display of fresh fruit and vegetables is over-whelming, especially in the major population centres of the East and West, most of the produce offered is not meant to be cooked, but to be eaten raw or in salads. In addition no crop can really survive in America unless it can be mechanically picked. This phenomenon has made herbs, some salad greens, and certain root vegetables outlandishly expensive.

The 'can' plays a considerable role in American food preparation. Few meals do not include a canned item, and virtually every foodstuff can be obtained in cans.

The supermarket shelves are also full of cardboard boxes stretching over hundreds of feet, filled with cake mixes (the shopper must 'just add water'), cookies, biscuits, crackers, dehydrated food, freeze-dried parsley and the like.

But the most distinctive aspect of the modern American supermarket is the frozen food chest, most of which covers an entire wall of the store. The huge frozen food firms get the pick of the crop; often it happens that the fresh produce is surplus and second best after the cannery and freezing plant are supplied. The greatest progress in frozen foods has been in freezing complete dishes, indeed complete meals. There are at least 250 different kinds of pre-cooked frozen foods on the market and, if all the varieties were included, the total might be 600. The frozen food chest is not only a perfectly splendid indicator of what Americans like eating, it is a very good representation of the dominant tastes in a given area. In one suburb of New York, where well-paid executives have their homes, the freezer chest carries a wealth of hors-d'oeuvre items, but there are no chitterlings. In a negro neighbourhood, chitterlings are carried, but smoked eel is not. In an Italian neighbourhood, lasagna is sold, but tamales are not.

Most large cities have natural food stores which sell chemical-free, unrefined, and special diet products. Interestingly, there is only one gastronomic magazine published in the United States, but at least five health food publications exist.

Having given the reader the general outline of the contemporary American cuisine, and the conditions from which it has evolved, we have in the first section of our text set out the listed dishes pertaining to the different regions, with, in most cases, a short description of them, and in the second section is given a widely representative selection of recipes. Clearly, it would not be practicable to give recipes for all the dishes mentioned in the first part of the book but there are recipes for all the dishes marked thus ◆. In addition, a number of recipes are given for dishes which are not indigenous to any particular region but are common to all; these are classified as 'All American'.

REGIONS

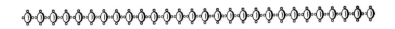

New England

Thus christened by an Englishman in 1614, New England remained under the influence of British Puritans for a long time. It is situated along the North Atlantic coast and includes the states of Maine, New Hampshire, Vermont, Massachusetts, and Connecticut; Boston is the major city. It is a rather mountainous region with numerous lakes; the climate is relatively cold and the winters hard.

Cold water fish abound, especially the cod and haddock which are among the culinary specialities. Maine's lobster, oysters, and clams are renowned.

New England cuisine is dominated by boiled dishes, puddings, porridges, breads and meats. In part, the circumstances in which the 102 English Puritans found themselves in 1620 dictated the use of moist heat cooking rather than frying or roasting. Boiled dishes can be made in a single vessel, with a minimum of attention. Lacking both labour and equipment, faced with incredibly difficult conditions, no domestic animals, and a miscellanea of game, roots and vegetables offered by the Indians, boiling might well have been the most expedient course.

In the early colonist, who expected to land in fertile warm Virginia, and instead landed in cold barren New England, we have a philosophical and political rebel, out of tune completely with a life of sensualism, indulgence and luxury. He was committed fully to whatever identified some centuries later as the Protestant ethic. In the modern New Englander, we have his spiritual heir, who takes pride in his thrifty asceticisms and self-denial.

A coincidence of inclination, circumstances and technology produced the New England cuisine. Continued affirmation of the values developed in those first moments of the successful colonization of the American continent, perpetuated it.

With this preface, some of the more peculiar foodways of New England are understandable. One custom which may be exaggerated concerns baked beans. The baked beans are prepared fresh for Saturday night supper, eaten again for Sunday breakfast with cod fish cakes, reheated for a noon meal and then make an appearance on Monday, Tuesday and Wednesday in various forms including the sandwich. Although the authors never encountered anyone who actually admitted this practice, people tell proudly of other individuals who were this extreme in their Yankee conservatism.

Baked beans along with the clambake, clam chowder and maple syrup production, have become symbols of New England. They are prepared differently in each of the states; peas, beans, kidney beans or yellow beans are used. In Connecticut, baked beans include onions while on the Cape Cod Peninsula, extending into the Atlantic from Massachusetts, cream is poured over the beans. In Vermont, citizens use maple syrup instead of molasses.

Traditionally, they are cooked in an earthenware pot. Despite the original reasons for the custom of beans on Saturday night – Puritans did not cook on the Sabbath – baked beans remain a popular Saturday night supper. Sunday features cod fish balls for breakfast and chicken fricassée for dinner. On Friday evening Cape Cod turkey (cod fish balls) is popular. Thursday is boiled dinner night, with leftovers making a reappearance as red flannel hash on Monday.

Even the clambake, which is the culinary spectacular of these parts, has the same rather low key flavour notes; it sounds much more interesting than the food actually is, featuring lobster, clams, fish, native sausage, corn, sweet potatoes. It is usually prefaced by a bowl of clam chowder consumed while the bakemaster prepares the bake. First a woodfire is built over rocks, then the embers and ashes are cleared away, seaweed is spread over the hot rocks and the layers of ingredients are placed over the steaming seaweed. A tarpaulin covers the food and it steams for about an hour.

The results are not always as intended. The fuel and the heat penetration are rather uncertain, and it is the unusual clambake that does not feature some raw items, and some completely over-cooked!

Clambakes are also available in 'take out' stores, and canned!

Another food rite that has become strongly identified with New England is gathering maple syrup, although few New Englanders have actually participated. Maple syrup has been made on the continent since pre-columbian times, and by white settlers of New England since about 1673. Some of the trees presently being tapped were saplings when the pilgrims arrived. Maple trees are extremely long lived and do not produce maple syrup until into their fortieth year.

A gash is made with an axe, then a hole bored with an auger into the tree. A spout or 'spile' is driven into the sugar hole on an upward slant to direct the sap into the hanging bucket. The average tree produces about 10 gallons of sap, which is boiled down to about $\frac{1}{4}$ gallon of syrup.

Buckets are emptied into a tank on a gathering sled which is driven to the sugar house for boiling down. The characteristic flavour and colour develop during the cooking process.

A much talked about event in New England is the 'sugaring off'. People sit around a table with bowls of snow before them and pitchers of hot syrup out of the boiling pot. The syrup is poured on top of the snow, and it is twirled 'like taffy' on a fork and eaten, with a dish of sour pickles and doughnuts.

Unlike sugaring off, which has little genuine significance, other than to the descendants of the original white Anglo-Saxon Protestant settlers, clam chowder is widely appreciated. A point of pride with homemakers and restaurateurs throughout the area.

Maine, which is closest to Newfoundland and the original Breton *chaudrée*, probably has the original clam chowder, made of whole soft shell clam, salt pork, clam juice water, potatoes and onion, seasoned with black pepper. Moving south, we find profuse variation of the basic recipe. In Massachusetts, milk is used, and the clams are chopped. In Connecticut, tomatoes are added to the Massachusetts recipe and aromatic seasonings are introduced. In New York the clam chowder, known as Manhattan, is made with ground clams, bacon instead of salt pork, flour thickening, tomato, garlic and aromatics. In the deep south, celery, okra, pimento and cayenne instead of black pepper enter the recipe.

One dish, more than a dish, a tradition, New England has given the rest of the country is the Thanksgiving Day meal, of turkey and garnishes, notably cranberry sauce, mashed turnips, succotash, relishes, pumpkin pie and cider. Legend has it that the Pilgrims celebrated the survival of some of their members, the fall after their arrival, with native foods supplied by the Indians. The native American turkey is, of course, gone from New England, although still present in the Southeast.

New England is a highly urbanized industrialized area which necessarily implies a drift away from traditional dishes. These days a good portion of the residents do not share these traditions and have other national origins, notably, Irish, Italian, and Portuguese. Yet New England tradition has been strong enough to moderate change. If some foods have changed, their basic spirit has not.

ANADAMA BREAD: A simple bread reputed to have been invented by a fisherman with a lazy wife who was obliged to do his own cooking, his bread making, etc. His bread-making job was often punctuated by frequent exclamations, among them: 'Anna, damn her!'

♦ APPLE CRISP: Sliced apples with a crumbly topping served with cream.

APPLE PANDOWDY, APPLE JONATHAN, APPLE BETTY: An apple pie that is baked in a deep ovenware dish. It is topped with biscuit dough instead of pie crust.

♦ APPLE PIE: A closed tart made of a very short dough, filled with apples that have been seasoned with cloves, cinnamon and nutmeg. Eaten with a wedge of cheddar cheese or with ice cream.

BAPTIST BREAD: Conventional bread but fried in deep fat.

BIRD'S NEST PUDDING: A name given to a variety of apple pudding. When made with a biscuit topping, it is called apple shortcake.

BLUEBERRY SLUMP: Blueberry dumplings served with cream. May also be made with apples. Blueberries are somewhat similar to bilberries, but blander in flavour.

BOAT STEERER: Clam fritters.

BOILED COD: Salt cod, soaked and boiled. Served with a Béchamel sauce into which a hard-boiled egg has been chopped.

♦ NEW ENGLAND BOILED DINNER: Corned beef that, unlike other corned beef in the United States, has not been cured with saltpetre but with coarse salt brine, and is therefore brown not red. Often boiled with vegetables and other meats and served with grated horseradish and johnny cake. (See p. 28.)

BOILED SALAD DRESSING: The traditional American salad dressing. It is a Béchamel sauce with egg yolks and seasoned with vinegar, a little sugar, salt and pepper. It has been largely replaced, first by mayonnaise and then by bottled salad dressings.

◆ BOSTON BAKED BEANS: Navy beans, salt pork, mustard, and molasses, baked togther in a narrow-necked earthenware pot.

BOSTON CREAM PIE: An interesting custard-filled pie made by baking a baking-powder-leavened crust, splitting it and filling with custard mixture.

BOSTON QUAIL: Cod fish cakes.

BROTHER JONATHAN'S HAT: A steamed pudding named after a Governor of the state of Connecticut.

BROWN BREAD BREVIS: Brown bread, a pudding-like steamed bread.

◆ BUTTERED LOBSTER: Diced lobster heated in butter with seasoning, served in vol-au-vent cases.

◆ CAPE COD TURKEY: Cod fish balls.

◆ CHICKEN-BROILED: Chicken basted with a vinegar mixture and grilled.

CHERRY BOUNCE: Black cherries preserved and eaten with New England rum.

CLAMBAKE: A method of steaming seafoods, chicken, etc., with seaweed in a pit lined with hot rocks. The name is often given to these foods, moist heated. Cooked together by more conventional methods.

◆ NEW ENGLAND STYLE CLAM CHOWDER: A soup, much like potato-leek, with the addition of clam juice and chopped clams.

CLAM PIE: A covered tart filled with poached clams.

COB APPLE PIE: The conventional deep-dish one-crust apple pie, made in an individual earthenware crock, but in this case served inverted, that is with the crust down.

COD TONGUES AND SOUNDS: Cod tongues, sounds (swim bladders) and cheeks are among the great delicacies of the world, simply poached and eaten with drawn butter. Few of these items ever get to market as they are consumed by the fishermen themselves on the fishing boats.

◆ CREAMED COD: Salt cod in a rich white sauce served on toast.

CONNECTICUT PIE: An apple pie unusual in that the apples are baked in a conventional two-crust pie; then the top crust and apples are removed, the apples seasoned and some returned in the bottom crust. The top crust is then replaced and covered with the remaining apple mixture. It is usually served warm with cream.

◆ CORN CHOWDER: A creamy soup of potatoes, corn, and cheese.

CROW'S NEST: See Bird's Nest Pudding.

DEACON PORTER'S HAT: A steamed pudding (also called Brother Jonathan's Hat). It is named after Deacon Porter, a trustee of the women's college, Mount Holyoke, in Massachusetts.

DOUGHNUT: A fried baking-powder-leavened dough product, flat and circular, with a hole in the middle. Much like a host of European fritters but for the hole. Whether this sophistication was an effort to reduce the greasiness of the product by better heat penetration, or a matter of convenience for New England seamen, who were said to have placed the doughnuts on the spokes of the wheels of their sailing vessels is a much argued point.

DOWN EAST PUDDING: A boiled pudding made from flour, molasses and blackberries. Usually served with brandy sauce.

EEL STIFFLE: A casserole dish not unlike scalloped oysters, made with eel, onions, potatoes and salt pork.

EEL PIE: Once a favourite dish, it has little popularity today. A double-crusted pie is filled with poached eels and oysters in a thin white sauce.

FISH CHOWDER: The word chowder is used for any hearty soup combining vegetables, seafood (clams, fish) with a salt pork base. It comes from the French word *chaudrée* by way of Newfoundland, Canada.

FLUMMERY: A cornstarch (cornflour) pudding with stewed fruit, eaten with heavy cream and sugar.

FOOL: A dish of stewed fruit with whipped cream and sugar.

FOURTH OF JULY DINNER: Menu eaten on the American

Independence Day: boiled salmon, peas, mashed turnips, mashed potatoes, biscuit shortcakes, strawberries and cream.

GAP 'N SWALLOW: Plum pudding with maple syrup.

GARDEN SASS: A folksy way of referring to vegetables, usually parsnips and corn.

GINGERBREAD: Much like the European breads and cakes of the same name, very popular since colonial times in New England.

GRAHAM CAKES: Small cakes of sour cream and graham flour leavened with soda and fried in a heavy skillet.

◆ GRUNT: A stewed berry or apple dish topped with a steamed dumpling.

HARTFORD ELECTION CAKE: Part of a New England traditional meal that features veal. It was a butter cake, yeast leavened, laced with wine, brandy and fruit – in essence a raised fruit cake.

◆ HARVARD BEETS: Small boiled beets, sliced and served in a thickened water and vinegar mixture.

HOLY POKES: Connecticut name for Baptist Bread. (See same.)

HUFFJUFFS: Maine name for Baptist Bread. (See same.)

◆ VERMONT STYLE INDIAN PUDDING: A milk pudding made with molasses, brown sugar and cornmeal.

◆ JAGASEE: A filling dish of beans, salt pork and peppers.

RHODE ISLAND JOHNNY CAKE: A traditional bread made simply of cornmeal, salt, water and milk, dropped on a hot griddle. Also made in other parts of the country in a pan (see MOUNTAIN) or in the ashes (then also called ash cables).

JOLLY BOYS: The small balls cut from the centre of doughnuts, fried in deep fat.

KEDGEREE: The familiar East Indian combination of rice, flaked cod and hard-boiled eggs brought to New England by sailing captains.

LOBSTER STEW: A small stew of lobster meat in a thin white sauce, seasoned with paprika and somewhat coloured by the lobster.

◆ MAPLE SYRUP FUDGE: A fudge of maple syrup and milk sometimes with nuts added.

MILK GRAVY: A simple gravy made by frying salt pork, sprinkling flour over it, and developing the sauce with milk. Used universally or eaten alone with biscuits.

MINCEMEAT PIE: An open or closed tart made with beef suet, neck meat, apples, quinces, citron, raisins, currants, molasses and seasoned with salt, cinnamon, allspice, nutmeg, pepper and cider.

◆ SCALLOPED OYSTERS

OYSTER STEW: Oysters poached in their own juice with butter. Combined with hot cream and milk, celery salt, salt, pepper, Worcestershire sauce and a dash of tabasco.

PARKER HOUSE ROLLS: Yeast dinner rolls, named after the Parker House, a Boston hotel, since 1855.

PICKLED EGGS AND RED BEETS: Once an exclusively Pennsylvania Dutch dish – hard-boiled eggs marinated in pickled beet juice, it has been taken up by Newport and Bar Harbour society – made with quail eggs.

PILGRIM CAKE: A simple flour paste, rolled out, coated with flour and cooked in hot ashes.

PAN PIE: A two-crust pie made with buttermilk, filled with salt pork and apples.

◆ POPOVERS: Light batter puffs.

◆ RED FLANNEL HASH: Corned beef (salted brisket), boiled potatoes, onions and beets, fried together and shaped like an omelette.

REPUBLICAN CAKE: A sponge cake leavened by cream of tartar and soda, flavoured with lemon extract.

SCRIPTURE CAKE: A colonial recipe that listed ingredients as references to the bible, for example: 2 cups Jeremiah 6:20, which turns out to be sugar.

SALT FISH DINNER: Traditional menu consisting of boiled salt fish, diced beets, boiled potatoes, milk gravy from salt pork, cottage cheese on corn bread.

◆ SHAD, BAKED: Whole shad stuffed and baked.

SHAKER DINNER: A dish that supposedly has its origins with the Shaker religious community but is widely popular in New England. Salt cod, boiled and garnished with boiled onions, fat salt pork, small potatoes and white sauce with chopped hard-boiled egg.

SHORE DINNER: A menu of fish chowder, pickles, celery, steamed clams, clam bouillon, lobster, potato chips, corn on the cob, tomato-lettuce salad and coffee.

SINGING HINNY: A pancake made from a dough leavened with baking powder, then fried on a griddle.

SNAP DOODLE: A coconut or chocolate covered butter cake baked in a flat square pan, cut in squares and eaten hot.

◆ SUCCOTASH: One of the few Indian dishes that have become part of the American repertory. Although originally made with whole pieces of corn on the cob, seasoned with bear fat, it endures only slightly modified as a mixture of lima beans and kernel corn.

TUMBLEOVER PUDDING: A plain pudding baked on top of stewed fruit, inverted before serving.

YALE BEETS: Small boiled and sliced beets, served in thickened orange juice.

TOGUS BREAD: A bread made basically of sweet milk and cornmeal, with sour milk and soda leavening with flour to bind it. It is sweetened with molasses and steamed. A Maine speciality coming from Togue – a French Canadian word of Indian origin.

WASHINGTON PIE: Not a pie but a butter cake that is baked in two pie tins, with raspberry jam between the layers.

YANKEE POT ROAST: A pot roast made with beef and root vegetables. Sauce is enriched with a veal foot that is boned and cut into the sauce.

Mid-Atlantic

Here we have the states of New York, Pennsylvania, New Jersey, Delaware, Maryland, and Virginia. The traditions are different in each of these regions. Those of the Pennsylvania Dutch will be treated elsewhere.

In New York's Long Island and in New Jersey we find many kinds of oysters including the Blue Point, the finest in America. Ducks and apples are particularly savoury.

In New York City, as in the bottom of a cauldron, the most incongruous elements are concentrated. Cooks for the most part American born spend a great amount of their time preparing specialities of other nations.

Philadelphia has the reputation of being refined. The city's customs, like its culinary traditions, developed in suburbs that profited from running alongside the country's first railroad, by laying in large stocks of goods.

The climate of Virginia and Maryland is rather mild and rainy. These particularly fertile regions are separated by the Chesapeake Bay. Plant and animal life are preserved in numerous parks. There is plumed fowl; in swampy regions buck, muskrats, frogs, terrapin tortoise. One variety of this last, the Diamond Black, about six inches long and weighing two pounds, is becoming rare as it cannot be raised in captivity. Trout, bass, and shad are caught in the rivers; sea bass, sea bream, salmon trout, grunters – a kind of hogfish, and the herring in the sea. Small blue crabs abound and are especially sought when they shed their shells. Oyster production is important but oysters here are large, a fact which explains the American habit of dousing them with ketchup or other sauces. Other methods of preparation are to fricasser, sauter, fry, pickle or bread them, to put them in pies or to serve them on toast.

The Mid-Atlantic region of America, in which her biggest portion and the nation's capital are located, has always faced east, towards Europe. It, more then any other section of the United States, is an extension of European society. Historically, it has been culturally dependent on England. Even after political independence, English mores and English cuisine dominated eating in this part of America. So intense was this affection for English ways, that many recipes which have passed from vogue in England, endure in nearly original form in America. Sally Lunn muffins and trifles of various types are good examples.

When the French cuisine became popular in England during the nineteenth century, it became equally popular among the rich and upper middle class in America, not independently, but through the intermediary of English acceptance. The chefs who introduced French foods to America, were in large part products of English hotels.

The basic English cuisine has been overlaid with other influences, notably Italian, Spanish, Jewish, Chinese and German. Some of these 'foreign' dishes have been so effectively assimilated that they could be claimed as regional cuisine.

For example, corned beef and cabbage, lox and bagels, vichyssoise, pizza, spaghetti, chow mein and chop suey (invented in America but Chinese in spirit), Spanish rice, all are common 'regional dishes'.

In rural areas there is more tradition but unlike the country people in other regions who are geographically isolated, here an incredible elaborate highway system ensures that almost everyone is exposed at one time or another to most dishes.

ARTICHOKE PICKLES: Refers to the Jerusalem artichoke not the globe artichoke; treated like turnip pickles.

BAKED ALASKA: A sponge base, topped with ice cream, masked with meringue and put under the grill to brown.

◆ BAY SCALLOPS: Small scallops taken inshore on Long Island. The part used – the adductor muscle – is slightly bigger then a sugar cube.

◆ BLUEBERRY MUFFINS: Served hot with butter.

BRIDGE CLUB SANDWICH: A triple decker sandwich of cream cheese, jelly, nutmeat and lettuce.

◆ BUCK AND BRECK: Mixed vegetables, pickled in cider vinegar.

◆ CHICKEN À LA KING: Cooked chicken in a white sauce, served with rice or in vol-au-vent.

◆ FRIED CHICKEN: Egg and crumbed, then deep fried.

CHURCH BUILDER CHICKEN: As the name implies, a popular dish for church suppers held for the building fund. A stew of chicken, cooked until it falls from the bone, with diced potatoes, lima beans, tomatoes and onions.

CHURCH SUPPER: Although the church supper has spread to other regions, it has its origin in the eastern settlements, which antedate other settlements. Originally, the church supper was simply communal eating. Each family brought its own meal and ate it at a communal table. It evolved and became a community project with each family assigned a specific dish.

◆ CIDER APPLE BUTTER: Apples cooked, sieved and boiled with cider until thick, then bottled.

CINNAMON BUNS: A yeast-aided dough, spiralled around raisins, syrup and cinnamon; browned on the bottom and toasted on top.

CLUB SANDWICH: A popular triple decker sandwich of sliced chicken, lettuce, mayonnaise, bacon and tomato.

COLESLAW: This is among the few Dutch recipes to endure from Colonial days. It is made of shredded cabbage with vinegar or cream dressings, elaborated in different regions with other vegetables, such as carrots or green and red peppers.

CRABURGER: A member of the burger family, a crab mayonnaise served on a hamburger roll.

CRAB FEAST: Refers to a meal of baked (on rock salt) or steamed crabs, liberally seasoned with peppercorns and red pepper, eaten traditionally on newspaper by hand, with beer, cheese and pickles.

◆ CRAB IMPERIAL: Actually a hot crab mayonnaise. A combination of choice backfin crab meat, mustard, Worcestershire sauce, mayonnaise, pimento, hard-boiled egg, heated in ramekins or shells.

CRAB NORFOLK: Lump crab meat treated *à la meunière*.

◆ DEVILLED CRAB: A mixture of mustard, butter, cracker crumbs, tabasco and crab meat, heated in shells or ramekins.

DIAMOND BACK TERRAPIN: Once household cooking of the

terrapin was as common as cooking chicken. Today, however, the high cost of terrapin, the prejudice of many people against reptiles and amphibia, and simple ignorance (few people know you can buy terrapin in New York), has made this a very rare restaurant dish. As far as we know, the only modern discussion of home preparation of a terrapin appears in a book by one of the authors of this volume.

DUTCH POTATOES: Peeled potatoes with a hollow centre, made with an apple corer, through which a sausage is passed. The potatoes are wrapped in fat bacon, packed and braised in a covered dutch oven (a kind of roasting dish which can be used on top of the stove) and finally browned under the grill.

FRIED MUSKRAT: Primarily a Maryland and Virginia dish; euphemistically called swamp rabbit. The muskrat is salted overnight, parboiled, then cut up like chicken, floured and deep fried.

FROZEN CUSTARD: This and frozen egg nog refer to ice cream of low fat and low egg content.

LADY BALTIMORE CAKE: A very light cake, quite similar to a light sponge, flavoured with rose water, filled and frosted with white honey icing and glazed fruits.

LOBSTER NEWBURG: Lobster cooked with wine, cream and paprika.

LOBSTER ROLL: A lobster mayonnaise served on a hot-dog bun.

LONG ISLAND DUCKLING: A domestic duckling of the Peking variety for the most characteristic flavour.

LOX AND BAGELS: Smoked salmon slices, on a toasted, circular, hard roll with a hole in the middle, made by first boiling and then baking bread dough.

MANHATTAN CLAM CHOWDER: A vegetable soup of tomatoes, green peppers, onions with clam broth and chopped clams.

MARYLAND EASTER HAM: A boiled ham which has been scored and green herbs placed in the slits. Cooked in a herb broth, wrapped in cheese cloth, cooled in the liquid and served cold with vinegar.

MARYLAND FRIED CHICKEN: Jointed chicken, floured, fried in butter, finished in the oven, served with sauce suprême, and garnished with strips of bacon.

OLIEKOEKEN: One of the few Colonial Dutch, as opposed to Pennsylvania Dutch, dishes still in the repertoire. A doughnut-like bread, well baked.
   The modern doughnut is an improvement as the hole in the middle allows better heat penetration and results in a crisper less greasy product.

OYSTERS CASINO: A popular restaurant dish, made with either oysters or clams, which would seem to be a professional contrivance rather than a native dish. The mollusc is placed on a bed of a pastry or cracker crumbs, covered with a square of bacon, and crossed strips of pimento.

◆ OYSTER FRITTERS: Coated with batter and deep fat fried.

◆ OYSTER STEW: A stew soup of oysters poached in their own liquid, butter, cream and Worcestershire sauce, tabasco and paprika.

OYSTER ROAST: Oysters roasted in the shell in the coals of a fire.

◆ PHILADELPHIA PEPPER POT SOUP: Soup made with tripe, veal knuckle, onions.

◆ PHILADELPHIA SCRAPPLE: Pork mixed with cornmeal and buckwheat flour, cooked, sliced and fried.

◆ PICKLED PEACHES: Whole peaches pickled with cider vinegar.

PLANKED SHAD: Planking is not very common these days. A fish or a steak is cooked on a well-seasoned white oak board that is kept specifically for that purpose and is eaten directly from the board.

◆ POTATO SALAD: Cooked potatoes in mayonnaise with onion, celery, green pepper and hard-boiled eggs.

PORTABLE SOUP: An old-time name for home-made bouillon, or more precisely, glace de viande.

◆ FRIED RABBIT: Joints of rabbit, egg and breadcrumbed, cooked in oven after browning.

◆ STUFFED ROCKFISH: Baked with a herb-flavoured stuffing.

RUSSIAN DRESSING: One of the many popular mayonnaise-based dressings. Mayonnaise, chilli sauce, chopped chives, pimentos, capers.

◆ SALLY LUNN: An old recipe for buns and yeast bread.

SARATOGA CHIPS: Paper thin potato chips attributed to a chef at the famous watering spot of the nineteenth century.

SENATE BEAN SOUP: The speciality of the United States Senate is a white bean soup seasoned with ham bone, chopped onion, chopped celery and garlic.

♦ SHAD ROE: The roe of the shad, grilled, baked or fried, served with cream sauce or bacon.

SMITHFIELD HAM: A type of cured ham identified with Virginia. Dried, cured and buried (theoretically) for a year. Quite excellent. Widely distributed at premium prices throughout the East and by mail to other areas.

SNAPPER SOUP: Although the only commercial company we found that packaged snapper soup was in the Midwest, canning soup from southern snapper, this is a popular dish in clubs and homes in the Mid-Atlantic. A treatment of snapping turtle (like terrapin) diced, simmered in butter, seasoned with nutmeg, and finished with egg yolk and cream.

♦ SPOON BREAD: An almost soufflé-like cornmeal mixture, spooned out of the dish and eaten hot with butter.

SOFT SHELL CRABS: Crabs caught in the act of leaving their shells, fried in a batter or sautéed. Entire crab can be eaten.

STEAMED CRABS: Crabs boiled in sea water and flavoured with bay, thyme, peppercorns, red peppers and dill.

♦ STRAWBERRY SHORTCAKE: Not a cake at all but rather a very short biscuit, split and sandwiched around stewed straw-berries and whipped cream, with more of the same on top.

SUBMARINE SANDWICH: A loaf of French or Italian bread with a cold meat filling.

TERRAPIN: Cooked until it can be removed from the shell and then cleaned and chopped and doused in sherry. It is returned to the shell, in which it is served.

THOUSAND ISLAND DRESSING: Another mayonnaise-based dressing: mayonnaise, chopped pimento, green pepper, chilli sauce, tomato ketchup, paprika, and chopped, hard-boiled eggs.

UPSIDE DOWN CAKE: Cake made with either peach halves or slices of pineapple. So called because the fruit is placed first in the pan and the batter poured in. After cooking the cake is turned over.

◆ VIRGINIA PEANUT SOUP: A cream soup made with chicken stock and peanut butter.

◆ BARBECUED WILD DUCK: Breasts grilled with a barbecue sauce.

The South

Still in the East but going South, we have North and South Carolina, Georgia, Florida, Alabama, Mississippi.

Along the Atlantic coast are salt water swamps and on the Florida side of the Gulf of Mexico, many small islands, the Florida Keys. Plant and animal life are those of both hot and tropical regions; among the many reptiles are alligators, lizards, salamanders, and some extremely poisonous snakes. In the lakes and rivers various bass, trout, catfish; in the sea different Mediterranean species: sea bass, mullets, sea bream, red mullet, dolphin, tuna, crabs, shrimp, oysters, and also shark and barracuda.

Tobacco and cotton are still grown but the latter in increasingly small amounts, its place given over to agriculture in Georgia and cattle in Alabama. Florida citrus fruit production has been expanding since the perfection of fruit juice canning methods.

A duality of value is present in the cuisine of the South. Some of the worst restaurant food in the United States is served below the Mason-Dixon line. Some of the finest cooking anywhere can be had in the homes.

The food of the country homes, which might as properly be called manors, is cooked almost entirely by black servants. The availability of labour has as dramatically affected this cuisine as the shortage of labour limited the New England cuisine. In the South, fried dishes predominate, some of which could properly be called sautés, in marked contrast to the boiled dish of New

England. Such foods as beaten biscuits have labour as a main ingredient. Imagine the time required to beat the dough for twelve biscuits, five hundred to a thousand times with a wooden mallet. As much manpower is expended making biscuits as chopping a tree or laying a section of railroad track. In the South, hot bread at meals is traditional. It is very interesting to note that although in the South more baking is done than in any other region, and government survey shows that half of Southern families have corn bread at least once a day, including urban families, less commercial mixes are sold in that area than elsewhere in the country, even among non-rural families. Southern families of all classes are less likely to buy bread than anywhere else.

It is an interesting but largely academic exercise to try to find African influences in the Southern cuisine. Compared to some other areas of the country, there are more hot tones, but compared to others namely the Southwest, Southern cuisine is as mild as a baby's kiss. While English influences are evident in the South, as well as French, Moravian, and Spanish influences, the African cuisine is not.

The early efforts of the slave holder to eliminate tribal identity and pride so as to preclude an insurrection were too effective for much if any of the African culture to endure. Even the availability to live off the land has been lost. In the so-called 'black belt' of the deep South, the area which was once devoted largely to cotton and is now machine farmed, where the negro deprivation is at its worst, people rely on manu-factured foods, even though between their shacks and the stores where they spend their few dollars for food are enough wild plants to feed the entire community.

A food event is the prime recreational activity in the South. Suppers are common and important events. Families picnic as a refreshing outing. Fund raising activities for local charities have a sure winner in a barbecue or a cake sale. Businessmen's groups which in other areas meet formally, or meet in restaurants for luncheons, often gather at night in the South at the local church to be fed family-style by the women of the community, who donate the food and turn the receipts over to some charity. Gifts of food are common. Neighbourliness is often expressed by offerings of a cake. Meals are social opportunities, elsewhere socializing is *post prandis*.

We have a situation in the South where communitism is still a valued part of the culture and eating has many of its historic significances. You cannot step into a home in the South, whether it is a mansion or a sharecropper's shack, without breaking bread, in some cases literally. It is absolutely impolite to refuse. A social faux pas equal to refusing a cup or glass of tea in an Arab's tent. Research in these circumstances requires the imbibing of vast quantities of home-made beer, usually in coca-cola bottles.

Many of the Southern states have dry counties. Mississippi was the last state to go wet, giving its counties local option as to whether alcoholic beverages would be sold. Many areas remain dry, mainly because the 'blackmail' taxes on illicit liquor are more profitable than the legalized taxes that would be levied.

Coffee is the usual social drink; where in other parts of the country people would have a cocktail or beer together, they have a cup of coffee in the South. Cola is an important beverage. The formula is much higher in stimulants in the South and the machines are everywhere, many still selling a bottle for six cents while in the rest of the country the price is ten or fifteen cents.

Other types of soda have a special market in the South. Southerners living in other areas will talk about a meal washed down with a particularly villainous red soda pop with the sort of affection people have for Château Lafite. In the South, buttermilk is an extremely popular beverage and can actually be found on menus as an alternative to coffee and tea. Unlike the buttermilk in other areas, which is a cultured skim milk something like a very loose yoghurt, much of the buttermilk consumed in the South is actually the by-product of butter-making, deliciously flecked with butter.

AMBROSIA: A dessert of oranges, apples, chopped pecans, grated pineapple, shredded coconut and cherries, served usually in a cut glass bowl, sprinkled with powdered sugar.

BAREFOOT BREAD: See Corn Pone (p. 59).

BATTER BREAD: Also called spoon bread. A very loose bread made with twice as much liquid as cornmeal, usually leavened by a reaction of buttermilk and baking soda.

◆ BRUNSWICK STEW: A thick chicken and veal stew, simmered with vegetables for several hours.

◆ BEATEN BISCUITS: The traditional bread of the plantation. A very simple dough of flour, lard and a little water, which was literally beaten with a rolling pin or mallet several hundred times until a great quantity of air was occluded in small uniform bubbles.

CAMP MEETING STEW: A stew of bacon, veal, chicken, pork, lamb, beef, onions, green pepper, okra, which is bound with flour, seasoned with black pepper, ketchup, cloves, allspice, tabasco, bay, etc. It was cooked and eaten at religious meetings.

CHICKEN HASH: Once a breakfast item in the South, this has become the staple of women's luncheons, to the considerable dismay of speakers on the lecture circuit. It is simply a chicken velouté with chopped leftover chicken in it.

◆ CHESS PIE: An open tart filled with custard of butter, sugar, corn syrup and pecan nuts.

43

CHICKEN SHORTCAKE: Creamed shredded chicken between slices of cornbread.

CHURCH OF GOD CORNBREAD: See Corn Pone (p. 59).

COQUINA SOUP: A periwinkle broth, simply made of periwinkle clams called coquina in Florida. They are cooked in water to cover and then sieved and served in the broth.

◆ CORNBREAD: In the early days of the country, an almost universal bread. The Southern variety differs from the Northern variety in the use of white cornmeal instead of yellow, and in the use of buttermilk instead of milk and the use of fat instead of butter.

◆ CORN PUDDING: A savoury sweet-corn and egg custard.

CORN DOGGERS: Corn pone baked in sticks.

◆ COUNTY CAPTAIN: A mildly curried chicken dish with almonds and currants.

CRACKLIN' BREAD: Cornbread made with drippings and renders of pork, salt, cornmeal and water.

CUBAN SANDWICH: A sandwich of Cuban inspiration, made of pieces of French bread, split, and then filled with meat and pickles, buttered and toasted in a special oven.

FISH FRY: Simply fried fish, either fresh or salt water, cooked at a community function.

FRIED MUSH: Cornmeal porridge, cooked, cut and fried. Usually eaten for breakfast.

FRIED PIES: Stewed fruit in a hard dough of flour, molasses, butter, eggs and milk, rolled thin and shallow fried.

GEORGIA PECAN PIE: A rich sweet custard mixture with pecan nuts in pastry shell.

GISPACK: The Florida rendering of Andalucian gazpacho.

GUINEA SQUASH: Another name for eggplant, which was also called bad apple.

HOE CAKE: A dough product made on a flat griddle or more romantically on a shovel, held over an open fire.

◆ HOPPING JOHN: A mixture of black-eyed peas, rice and ham.

◆ JAM CAKE: A butter cake made in a tube pan, with blackberry jam, an old North Carolina recipe.

KRAWLS OR CRAWLS: Refers generally in Key West, Florida, to turtles which are treated like veal cutlets.

LEATHER BRITCHES: Name given to green beans which have dried on a string and cooked like dried beans with salt pork.

LIGHT RED HORSE BREAD: A very thin cornmeal bread which is fried in deep fat. It is popular in South Carolina with fish suppers.

LIMPING SUSAN: Rice and okra combination.

MOCK CHICKEN: A name given to a variety of preparations of pork, beef or veal which has been treated as though the main element is chicken. For example: Mock Chicken Salad is made of mayonnaise, celery, diced pickles, etc., but with pork instead of the more usual chicken.

MOLASSES PIE: An open tart, filled with a custard, molasses and buttermilk.

OKRA SOUP: Okra cooked in beef stock with bacon stock and onions.

OLD SOUR: A hot sauce made in Key West, Florida, of lime juice seasoned with bird peppers (*Capsicum baccatum*).

PALMETTO SALAD: The sliced cabbage palm leaf-bud, which is widely used by rural natives. It looks like a Chinese cabbage. Often using the bud means killing the cabbage palm tree.

◆ PEACH CRISP WITH HARD SAUCE: Peaches cooked gently with a rolled oat topping.

PEANUT BRITTLE: A peanut toffee.

PHILPY: A hot rice bread made in the state of South Carolina.

◆ PIEDMONT DOVE: Casserole of doves, squabs, pigeons or other small game.

PILAU: This is, of course, a corruption of the word pilaf and is just that. There is Okra Chicken Pilau, made of South Carolina long-grain rice, which is quite excellent.

PINE BARK STEW: A small stew of fish, bacon, onions, butter, ketchup and water.

PLANTAIN CHIPS: A Key West, Florida, treatment of cooking

bananas by deep frying them to resemble potato chips. It is of Cuban inspiration.

◆ PLANTATION DINNER: Ham cooked with parsnips and sweet potatoes.

POKE SALAD: A salad of dandelions, pig weed, turnip greens and land cresses.

POMPEY'S HEAD: A fairly popular dish which is actually a meat loaf of ground beef and salt pork roughly moulded into the shape of a head.

POSSUM AND SWEET TATERS: A folksy way of referring to a dish of roast opossum and sweet potatoes.

RICE PEAS: Small peas, so tender they can be cooked in the pod.

SHORTNIN' BREAD: A rich bread, made simply of flour, brown sugar and butter, developed like a sponge cake.

SHE CRAB SOUP: A cream of crab soup with added interest of the clam roe. The speciality of Charleston, N.O.

SHRIMP JAMBALAYA: A stew of shrimps, oysters, ham and chicken with seasoning, garnished with raw vegetables such as scallion and celery.

SHRIMP PASTE: Shrimp paste is a compound butter introduced into the area by French Huguenots.

SMOKED MULLET: A speciality of St. Petersburg, Florida, which is a gourmet delicacy.

♦ SOUTHERN FRIED CHICKEN

SOUR ORANGE MARMALADE: A speciality of Florida where the bergomat orange grows.

SPIDER CORNBREAD: Cornbread cooked in a heavy iron skillet or spider (a pan with detachable legs) over an open fire.

STUFFED SWEET POTATOES: Baked and stuffed with crisp bacon and onion.

SWEET POTATO PIE: An open tart filled with a custard mixture of sweet potatoes which have been seasoned with allspice, mace, cinnamon and the like.

SYLLABUB: A rich beverage of sweet wine, heavy cream and powdered sugar.

SYONE CRABS: An excellent boiled crab from the Gulf of Mexico, eaten widely in Florida and other gulf states.

TUPELO HONEY: A honey from the tupelo gum trees in West Florida that is of a light amber colour.

TURTLE LIVER PASTE: A dish quite like foie gras, without any fishy taste, that is eaten in some Florida communities.

♦ WILD DUCK: Stuffed with orange, apple and celery, sherry, then roasted.

Creole

Ten flags have flown over Louisiana and the surrounding territory: the Spanish flag of Leon and Castile, carried by Columbus and DeSoto; the Fleur-de-Lis raised by LaSalle; the flag of Bourbon Spain; the Union Jack; the French Tricolor; the United States flag of fifteen stars and stripes; the Lone Star flag of West Florida Republic; the Stars and Bars of the Confederate States of America; the flag of Independent Louisiana; and the present United States flag. The influences of other groups is apparent in the cuisine, if not in the political history of the area. The Acadians, of French ascendance, expelled by the English from the Acadian peninsula of Canada (present day Nova Scotia) in 1755, settled a decade later in New Orleans. They have half a million descendants in present-day Louisiana. The blacks brought to America as slaves, in this area managed to keep some identity. The original Indians have left a culinary legacy. German immigrants made a small contribution. Anglo-Saxon Americans introduced other regional dishes during the eighteenth century when they were moving into the Southwest from earlier eastern settlements.

The French, creoles, who came through the West Indies with a spicy flavour profile provided by the Spanish and African cuisines, dominate this culinary amalgam. The Cajuns, descendants of the French Acadians, especially those who live in the black country of the area, maintain a much purer tradition than the English majority in Southern Louisiana.

Just as one can hear occasionally beautiful spoken archaic French along with the local patois, in the Cajun kitchen one sometimes finds a purely French dish, unassailed by other influences.

Unfortunately, modern highways now bring these back areas more under the control of the non-French majority. Much of this uniquely wonderful culture, including the continued use of French, is being systematically rooted out by the state government, which is bent on incorporating the Cajun into an Anglicized Louisiana. It may eventually come to pass that the only living pure culture of the Cajun will be the cuisine.

Much of the genuine Cajun cooking involves fish and fresh crustaceans. Louisiana has over two million acres of inland water, an acre for every inhabitant. Although crawfish abound in other areas, nowhere else are they systematically fished and eaten. In some areas, they are a secondary crop in the rice fields. Cajun and some non-Cajun gather them with a creole crawfish net, which is actually a mini- Chinese lift net. The delicious river shrimp are caught by an even more unusual method in the back country bayou (swamp rivers). Small bundles of willow or wax myrtle twigs are weighted in the water with the foliage down. The shrimp rest in the bush and are then shaken into a dip net. Crabbing and castnetting for shrimp are also semi-sports that provide plenty of delicious seafood for the Cajun table.

The swamps abound with small game and almost every migratory fowl represented in America, and these provide another important meat in the Cajun diet, even when they have to be poached.

Creole cooking is distinguished from the food of the rest of the country by the side use of aromatics; bays, parsley, thyme, onion tops, garlic, shallots, basil, cloves, allspice, chervil, burnet, savory, tarragon, etc.

The restaurants of New Orleans, specifically Antione's, Arnauds, Brennans, Belmonico, Galatoire's, Broussards, all have become American culinary shrines, but the real gastronomic delights of this city are in the working man's cafés and bars, where such dishes as red beans and rice, and steamed crayfish and shrimp, have a transcendent quality.

This is the signal difference between this region and the rest of the country; the labourer, even the black dock worker who trundles huge bales of cotton all day, eats well and loves good food.

The joie de vivre that gave America jazz and keeps the carnival alive in Protestant North America, prevails here in culinary matters.

BAYOU TECHE: A sort of buttermilk pancake.

BOEUF-BURGERS: This is the familiar American hamburger, gallicized New Orleans style.

BOUILLABAISSE: Of course the principle is the same as the Marseillaise version, but the fish is different, usually gaspergou, red fish, or red snapper, and so is the seasoning, garlic but no saffron.

CAFÉ BRÛLOT: Cloves, cinnamon, lemon peel, sugar and cognac combined in a bowl, flambéed, and then moistened with expresso coffee.

◆ CALAS: Fried rice cakes, seasoned with vanilla, nutmeg and cinnamon. A popular confection in New Orleans for Sunday morning breakfast.

CHAURICE: This is the Creole corruption of the word Chorizo, for a hot Spanish sausage.

◆ COURT-BOUILLON: While the origins of this word are obvious, the name now refers to a dish of boiled fish.

◆ CRAB AND OKRA GUMBO: Thick mixture, something between a soup and a stew, served over rice.

◆ CRAYFISH STEW: Spicy crayfish mixture, with spring onions and parsley.

CRAYFISH BISQUE: A traditional French *bisque d'écrevisse*.

◆ SPICED CRAYFISH: Crayfish boiled in spiced liquid, eaten chilled.

CUSHAWS: A sort of pumpkin with a neck, which is parboiled and then cooked with a caramel butter glaze.

◆ CUSH-CUSH: A mush of cornmeal, baking powder and milk, eaten as a porridge. Also called couche-couche; might well be a corruption of N. African Cous-cous.

DAUBE GLACÉ: The familiar French daube, unnecessarily called glacé. It is, however, much more highly seasoned than in France.

◆ FISH GUMBO: A gumbo based on white fish with tomatoes and okra.

FILÉ: A ubiquitous creole seasoning of dried sassafras powder. See Sassafras (pp. 55 and 56).

GATEAU SIROP: A gingerbread-type cake made with cane syrup.

◆ GRILLADE PANNÉ: A breaded slice of round of veal, fried.

GUMBO: A soup which includes *filé* (powdered sassafras). Admits every conceivable version.

GUMBO D'HERBES: Spelled many ways, includes Gumbo dez'Herbes; generally a gumbo which includes mustard greens.

HOT STUFF: Folksy way of referring to the very popular flavoured vinegars and pepper sauces.

LA COLLE: Molasses and peanut candy in paper cases.

◆ JAMBALAYA: An umbrella term for any pilaf-like combination of rice and other ingredients; seafood, black beans, fish, meats, etc.

◆ MAQUE-CHOUX: Corn scraped from the cob and cooked in oil with seasoning and onions.

MIRLITON: A dish of vegetable pears stuffed with crab, shrimp and sausage.

◆ NEW ORLEANS RICE: Rice with a sauce of shrimp, peas, tomatoes.

◆ OREILLE DE COCHON: Deep-fried dough twisted in the shape of pig's ears.

◆ OYSTER LOAF SANDWICH: Other East coast regions claim this delicacy but chances are it originated in New Orleans. A loaf of French bread is hollowed out and filled with fried tiny oysters and melted butter.

◆ OYSTERS ROCKEFELLER: The specialty of Antoine's restaurant in New Orleans, supposedly made up of over thirty 'secret' ingredients, but basically a poached oyster replaced in the shell, filled with anise-flavoured spinach purée, covered with *sauce Mornay*.

POMPANO EN PAILLOTE: Another specialty of Antoine's of

New Orleans, a pompano fillet cooked with seasoning and garnished in a paper case.

POTATOES O'BRIEN: Not a regional dish but like so many other restaurant dishes created in New Orleans, it has become popular in the home there and around the country. Basically squares of potatoes are deep fried and combined with pimentos.

◆ POOR BOY SANDWICH: The origins of this dish are pleasantly obscure. It is said the word originated with the French *pourboire* in French-speaking New Orleans. An alternative explanation suggests that young boys solicited food from restaurateurs, asking if they didn't have something for a poor boy, and were given a huge sandwich made of a whole loaf of French bread, with meat, cheese, mustard. Today, a poor boy sandwich can be of any filling although the French bread is still used. In other areas, the 'poor boy' is called a 'submarine' because of its shape, or a 'hero' because of the courage needed to consume an entire one alone. Hero, in areas influenced by the foodways of Italians, are often hot sandwiches of meatballs, sausage and peppers with tomato sauce.

PRALINE: A candy made with simple crystals, something like fudge or fondant. Can have coconut, pecans or chocolate as additional elements.

◆ RED BEAN PURÉE: Soaked and boiled beans puréed and cooked with onions and seasonings.

ROUX: The origin of this word in French cuisine is quite apparent, yet roux in Creole cooking takes on added dimensions in that besides the flour and fat combination, vegetable elements and seasonings are added so that the roux becomes a vehicle.

SAUCE ARNAUD: The house specialty of a famous New Orleans restaurant; much like sauce rémoulade but with plenty of horseradish.

♦ SAUCE REMOULADE CREOLE: Quite different from the original French version in that it emphasizes New World ingredients: mustard, horseradish, white vinegar, anise, tomato purée, paprika, cayenne pepper, garlic, onion purée, chopped parsley, pimentos, olive oil and puréed celery!

♦ SHRIMP CREOLE: Shrimp in a tomato sauce with onion and pepper.

♦ SHRIMP GUMBO: A gumbo incorporating shrimp, okra and onion.

SOFT SHELL TURTLE STEW: A small stew of turtle meat (not terrapin) with sherry and seasonings.

STUFFED PEPPERS: Stuffed with crab combined with mayonnaise and chilli sauce.

TAC-TAC: Popcorn (that is a special type of kernel corn which expands or pops to thirty times the size when heated), covered with caramel.

TABASCO: A specific brand of pepper sauce made of tiny red bird peppers in vinegar on Avery Island, after an old family recipe. Now, generally refers to any hot pepper sauce. The original pepper bush seeds are reputed to have come from Tabasco, Mexico.

SASSAFRAS: Bush of the Laurel family from which *filé* is made: the powder made from young dried sassafras leaves that gives a subtle aroma to stews and soups. It was first prepared by 'boboshillies', old squaws of the Choctaw tribe on the Bayou Lacombe reservation, who sold it in the old quarter of New Orleans. *Filé* is added to dishes at the last minute and should never be boiled.

Mountain

Mountain cuisine is quite similar to cuisine identified with the black American i.e. Soulfood. Both are based on the same products and evolve from economic necessity: the need to use the least expensive foods.

In these states of Kentucky, Tennessee, West Virginia, Missouri and Arkansas we expect insular culture and we find it; a way of life with its own distinct values and traditions. The Appalache Mountains are the spine of the South East. Mountain people are apart from the civilization that surrounds them, whether the mountains are the Massif-Central, the Himalayas, the American Smokies, Allegheny Mountains or the Ozarks. These areas are partly set apart by economic factors; they are infertile, unindustrialized, with their main resource, coal, redundant today. Here is the largest concentration of non-black poor in the United States. Relative prosperity came to the rest of the South and the Midwest a century ago. Cash crops, and industry, bought luxuries, but the mountains, isolated both culturally and geographically, never quite made it into the twentieth century.

People live in the mountains as the early pioneers and settlers lived, eating 'hog and hominy', using word and speech patterns that have passed from the common vocabulary of most Americans generations ago. They maintain a code of the hills, and the clannish social order that is completely irrelevant today except to them. Mostly they are pure Anglo-Saxon stock. English, Irish, Scottish, they are the archetype of the lean, lanky American of colonial literature, now largely over-whelmed by people of continental origin in other areas.

There is little money to buy goods. Despite fish and game laws which have recently been passed, a great deal of the diet is made of small game and fish, taken in season and out. Wild plants, nuts, fruits and berries supplement the staples of corn products and pork. Pigs rummage in a semi-wild state for acorns and roots, and are smoked, cured and rendered at home.

One cannot really romanticize the mountain cuisine; it is too bland to have many aesthetic virtues. Cooking methods are understandably primitive. Since much meat is cured or smoked, water cooking is common. Tough game animals are dealt with as a simple stew. Abundant fat makes fried food common. Elaborate cakes with white flour are not very frequent desserts. Native berries lend themselves more to pies. The hot breads that typify Southern cuisine are, of course, absent.

Some progress has been made in some areas. In the thirties, the massive Tennessee Valley Authority brought cheap power to the area, created jobs, and focused governmental interest on the region. Television, which is the concomitant of electricity, has opened something of the outside world and made people somewhat more receptive to changes in diet.

As might well be imagined, there are no mountain-food restaurants. The traditional recipes found in the homes are based on immediate economics. One product, country ham, has had some national penetration. It is, however, a gourmet item that cannot have been sampled by more than a fraction of the general population. Most people find these dry-cured hams rather dry and strong, which precludes its becoming a national item.

◆ BACKBONE WITH NOODLES: Pork backbone stewed with onions and served with noodles.

BEAN POT ROAST: A sort of daube with meat and onions cooked in a bean pot, which is traditionally buried in a bean hole. (A hole dug in the ground to size, lined with stones, which are heated by a wood fire.) The pot is buried and cooks by the heat of the stones.

BLACKWALNUT SOUP: A chicken velouté garnished with black walnuts and whipped cream.

◆ BRUNSWICK STEW: A very popular mountain stew that is simmered for at least twenty-four hours in a black iron hog skinning kettle, until it is almost homogeneous. Made of small game, local vegetables, old fowl, etc.

◆ BUCKWHEAT CAKES: Buckwheat and wheat flour mixed to a batter with yeast and baked in a griddle.

BURGOO: A specifically Kentucky version of Brunswick Stew, made traditionally in giant 50-gallon American cauldrons used for skinning hogs. Goat, corn, tomatoes, red and black pepper, available domestic and wild game, and squirrels often comprise the ingredients.

◆ BUTTERMILK BISCUITS: A hot biscuit often served at lunch.

BUTTER BEANS: The local word for lima beans.

◆ FRIED CATFISH: Coated with egg and cornmeal and fried in bacon fat.

◆ CHITTERLINGS OR CHITILLINS'S: The small intestine of swine, cleaned and parboiled, then deep fried.

CORN PONE: A corn bread enriched with molasses.

CORNMEAL MUSH WITH PORK: Cooked pork mixed with cornmeal mush, chilled, sliced and fried.

◆ CRACKLING BREAD: Another corn bread using cracklings left after rendering down fat.

CREAM POTATOES: The local term for mashed potatoes.

CYMLINGS: Refers specifically to the scallop small squash, popular in the area, but can refer to others, such as yellow sommuter, south patty pan squash. The Zucchini and Hubbard squash varieties popular elsewhere are not often seen.

DERBY BREAKFAST: Part of an elaborate ritual at Louisville, Kentucky, during the annual running of the Kentucky Derby, the most prestigious horse race. Any and all regional specialities are served, plus mint julep.

DRIED SWEET POTATOES: Among the many vegetables, including corn and string beans, dried in the summer to keep for the winter.

EGG BUTTER: A sort of jam made of sorghum syrup (p. 62), heated in a skillet, mixed with beaten eggs and a little nutmeg. Made in the spring, when the preserves put up the fall before are running out.

ENGLISH PEA: The common green garden pea, so called to differentiate it from black eyed peas.

FATBACK: Name given to the fatty portions of bacon, used as a cooking fat and universal seasoning.

FIELD BEANS: Green beans, called string beans elsewhere.

FRIED PIE: A semi-circle of pastry filled with a cooked sweet fruit mixture and fried with fat in a skillet.

◆ FRIED GREEN TOMATOES: Slices dipped in cornmeal and fried in bacon fat.

GARDEN LETTUCE: The soft variety of lettuce, seldom favoured in other parts of the country.

GOOBER: Local name for peanuts (ground nuts).

GREEN APPLE PIE: Traditional American apple pie but made with small sour apples.

◆ GREEN BEANS: Bacon in the piece cooked slowly with green beans.

GREENS: Refers to all types of salad greens except dandelion and beets, which are not much favoured.

◆ GRITS: Hominy broken into small particles.

◆ HAM BONE SOUP: Ham bone and scraps simmered with tomatoes, potatoes and onions.

HOG AND HOMINY: The way local people refer to their diet, which consists largely of pork and corn products.

HOG JOWL, GREENS, POT LIKKER AND CORN PONE: Hog jowl baked with greens, served with cornmeal dumplings.

HOMINY: White Indian corn with the hull removed, broken into uniform sized particles. Also called grits when in small particles.

◆ HOMINY AND BACON: Hominy grits baked with vegetables and bacon.

◆ HUSH PUPPIES: Bits of corn batter, traditionally fried in the fat used for frying fish. So called because they were thrown to the dogs to quiet them while the meal was cooking.

HYPOCRITE PIE: A pie shell, partially filled with stewed dried mashed peaches, topped with a custard mixture.

IRISH POTATOES: The common white potato, so called to differentiate it from the sweet potato which is quite popular.

JEFF DAVIS PIE: Jefferson Davis was the president of the Confederate States of America during the Civil War. An open pie filled with custard mix.

JOHNNY CAKE: A cornmeal batter cake, usually served with maple syrup.

KENTUCKY HAM: Country ham, dry rub cured rather than soaked. Sugar and salt are rubbed in the ageing ham throughout the ageing process. Unlike Virginia ham, it is not buried. Usually boiled as a preliminary process.

'LASSES: A shortened form of the word molasses, which actually refers not to molasses but to sorghum, a honey coloured syrup made from a corn-type plant and not from the sugar cane (which is made into commercial molasses).

LYE HOMINY: Hominy (which is whole, dehulled white Indian corn) alkaline treated to remove the rough fibrous outer coat.

◆ NECK BONES AND CORN MUSH: A corn and pork meat loaf, cut into slices and fried.

MINT JULEP: A traditional drink of Kentucky, made of bourbon, simple syrup and cut mint (not crushed), over fine crushed ice.

◆ OATMEAL PIE: Filling of oatmeal, walnuts, corn syrup, spiced with cinnamon.

◆ FRIED OKRA: Sliced, rolled in cornmeal and fried.

PEACH CHIPS: Peach slices, which have been sugared and drained and are then glazed in boiling sugar and sun dried on sugar covered boards.

PEARL HOMINY: A large-size grit, known as samp.

PERSIMMON PUDDING: The most regional of mountain desserts. Made of the much smaller American variety of persimmon, deep orange in colour and about one-and-one-half inches in diameter, gathered and eaten only after the first killing frost; otherwise they are too tart. Often the pudding is made with cornmeal and sweet potatoes as a base.

◆ PICKLED PIG'S FEET: Simmered in spiced vinegar, served cold.

PICKED FISH: This is a very old recipe, actually more of a device than a recipe, which probably had Indian origins. It is nearly impossible to make a decent meal of fried fish caught in most streams as they cannot be filleted and are more bones than meat. In picked fish the fresh-caught fish is parboiled and then filleted. The meat is breaded and fried or used in a dish.

POKE SALAD: A green salad of poke weed.

POT LIKKER: The liquid left over from the cooking of vegetables, usually greens, and meat.

RAMPS: Wild garlic roots, fried in a skillet with bacon grease for about twenty minutes, flavoured with salt and vinegar.

RAZORBACK: A very excellent type of wild pig with an extremely sweet flesh.

EYE GRAVY: The gravy developed from the drippings of fried ham, often moistened with coffee.

SIMMON BEER: A fermented beverage made from persimmon and cornmeal mixed together, baked in loaves and in wooden tubs. Can be drunk in a week.

◆ SALT PORK WITH MILK GRAVY: Pork simmered then fried and served with a white gravy.

SALT RISING BREAD: Really little justification for the name. Actually bread is made on a cornmeal base utilizing wild yeasts or bacteria as the source of leavening gas.

SAMP: See Pearl Hominy.

SKILLET CORN: Kernels of corn scraped from the cob and cooked with bacon, bacon fat, sliced onion and a little water in a skillet.

◆ SOUR RIBS: Spareribs basted with a sweet-sour marinade.

SOURWOOD HONEY: An attractive honey from Tennessee.

SQUIRREL PIE: The squirrel is a staple food in all forms of the mountains. Every boy has his squirrel rifle and hunts these attractive rodents.

STAKE CAKE: A wedding cake, made by stacking layers brought by the individual guests.

◆ SMOTHERED CHICKEN: Cooked in oven with milk.

SWAMP RABBIT: Muskrat cooked in a stew.

TATERS: Refers specifically to the sweet potato as opposed to the white potato which is called an Irish potato.

◆ MASHED TURNIPS: Turnips cooked slowly with salt pork, then mashed.

◆TURNIP GREENS: Bacon cheek simmered with greens.

WATER-GROUND MEAL: This is the staple cereal food of the mountains. It is white flint corn ground between stone mill-stones.

WATERMELON SWEET PICKLES: Pickled watermelon rind, among the most popular relish of the region.

SPICED BEEF ROUND: Originally a Mid-Atlantic dish of round of beef, but much more popular in the cities of the mountain region as a Christmas meal. Larded with pork fat; cured with salt, pepper, brown sugar, vinegar, spices; sim-mered, cooled, glazed with brown sugar and eaten in small, thin wedges.

Midwest

The Midwest is the heart of the North American continent, literally and figuratively. It is a geographic phenomenon unique in the world that has given rise to a culture phenomenon equally unique. No other continent has a land mass this far from the sea densely populated and so developed.

The natural setting of the Midwest has contributed mightily to its uniqueness. The Mississippi River system and its watershed, and the great lakes – the largest freshwater system in the world – plus hardwood forests and extensive prairies, as well as extraordinary climate that is suited to the producing of high yield crops, have combined to make this the outstanding agricultural land of the world.

There may be other areas with this kind of agriculture potential on an acre by acre basis, but nowhere is there that much first-quality farm land in one continuous belt.

Into this setting came a rather special group of people, internal immigrants, uniformly bourgeois in their outlook, religious, conservative, hard working, and (most important), people who for one reason or another could not make a go of it in the eastern and southern settlements where mineral resources were quickly depleted and free land unavailable. They loaded their families on Conestoga Wagons, and streamed into this land through the Cumberland Gap, isolating themselves by eight-hundred miles from the seaboard culture.

They welcomed, as no other immigrants to this continent have been welcomed, the North European and German immigrants that followed them into the Midwest. Despite their difference of culture and language, their philosphy incorporated the cardinal virtues of the Midwesterner and the abiding belief in hard physical work. Work has always been, and still is, the focus of existence. Other peoples seek to escape labour, especially manual labour. The Midwesterner fundamentally relishes it. Earning a living by the sweat of your brow, tilling the soil of your own land, are consummate ends.

The culture which grows from these circumstances, in this land, with these people, has become strongly identified with the United States of America. If there is such an animal as a *homo americanus*, he lives west of the Appalachians and east of the Rockies. While the coastal areas are extensions of the European society, the Midwest is America, insulated, isolated, insular and isolationist. The people you identify on the streets of London or Paris as Americans are Midwesterners. They do not care that you know it, and there is no reason why they should. Their triumph over nature and adversity makes them a chosen people.

A European plunging into the Midwest by jet plane cannot really comprehend it. The climate is hot and humid in the summer; viciously cold in the winter. The landscape undulating monotonous fields. The people, provincial and industrious, in a classless society, are alien to him. He finds few minority groups and few minority ideas to disturb the equanimity of prosperity. He finds little concern for the outside world and small interest in foreign food except of course the Norwegian, German and Dutch food that is part of the Midwestern culture.

There may be a good Italian or French restaurant somewhere in the Midwest, but we did not find it. Steak houses, buffet restaurants, diners and drive-ins satisfy the Midwesterner. He wants simple food and a lot of it. Nothing typifies this area more than the annual Mother's Day dinner in the Hotel Lemington in St. Paul, Minnesota. (Mother's Day is, of course, a Midwestern invention.)

It is held in a vast auditorium called the Hall of States, which seems large enough for an indoor horse race. This arena is filled with buffet tables, twenty or thirty feet long, loaded with hams, rounds and ribs of beef, turkey, geese, whole fish, dozens of varieties of vegetables, an immense quantity of baked goods, mammoth bowls of salads . . . without exaggeration, thousands of pounds of prepared foods. People pay two dollars to eat whatever they want, as much as they want, and hundreds are accommodated. The most amazing part of this phenomenon is that not one drop of beer, wine or alcohol is available and no one seems to miss it.

All this food, and most of the food in the Midwest is prepared in the most direct manner: meats are roasted, vegetables are water-cooked. Few seasonings are used, almost no aromatics except sage in stuffing. Flavour interest must be in the food itself (most of it is absolutely first quality), and in the various pickles, condiments, and relishes which accompany it.

Among the factors that contribute to this 'flavour profile' is the Northern European influence. Fats are used in the Midwest rather than oils for cooking purposes, because this was the custom in Northern Europe. Another factor is the suitability of this diet to the Midwestern way of life. Hard work demands a high level of nutrition, including steak and eggs for breakfast. Circumstances have also conspired to make the cuisine rather monotonous. In the early days, there was not very much money for buying spices, and other luxury goods, from the coast and hauling them out to the Midwest.

Intensive farming fairly well eliminated natural vegetation. People were, in other words, limited to what they could grow: good beef, good corn, good vegetables. They saved such imported luxuries as oranges for Christmas presents.

This same simple diet has continued because the people like it. They are conservative in their politics and equally conservative in their food habits.

AMERICAN CHEESE: This and a variety of other names (rat cheese, store cheese, coon cheese), refers to a cheese made by the Cheddar process.

◆ ANGEL FOOD CAKE: A cake made in a specially-designed mould and given its particular appearance and flavour by a disproportionately high amount of egg whites to flour.

APRICOT LAYER LEATHER: Fruits such as apricots, peaches and plums, spread on waxed paper to sun-dry and form a leather-like sheet.

BANANA SPLIT: An ice cream dessert with the mounds of ice cream, which may number up to 30, placed between bananas sliced the long way. The entire mixture is covered with syrups, candied fruits, nuts and whipped cream.
   Eating 30 scoops of ice cream is a thing of pride among teen-agers.

BEAN SUPPER: A social evening sponsored by some local group, in which beans and cornbread are the main victuals.

BLACK BEAN SOUP: Soup of beans made with ham, onions, carrots, thyme and bay.

BOOYAW: This is a corruption of the word 'bouillon', which snuck over the border from French Canada. Usually, it is a very hearty soup, not a bouillon at all.

BROASTED CHICKEN: A type of fried chicken in which the frying process is done in a specially-designed, closed, deep fryer under pressure.

◆ BROWNIES: Delicious chocolate and walnut cookies.

BUFFET: This is the Midwest equivalent of the Farwest smorgasbord, a way of dining in a restaurant without service. All the food is laid out on a central table, which may be elaborate enough to have hot and cold sections built in, and the diners serve themselves and eat as much as they want for a *prix fixe*.

BUTTERMILK SHERBET: Buttermilk and crushed pineapple, sweetened and frozen.

CANTALOUP HONEY: A preserve made from cantaloup melons spiced with nutmeg and served as a jam.

CHAR-BROILED: A rather bizarre way of cooking steaks that combines the worst features of broiling and charcoal cooking, in that the steaks are cooked over a gas-fired pumice composition bed of coals.

◆ CHEESE FRITTERS: Ementhaler cheese dipped in batter and deep fat fried.

◆ CHEESE DROPS: Small, light savouries.

◆ CHICKEN SALAD: Diced chicken tossed with celery, green pepper and mayonnaise then chilled.

CHICKEN POT PIE: Chicken in a light Béchamel sauce.

◆ CORN CHOWDER: Thick soup with salt pork, corn and potatoes.

CORN-FED BEEF: American beef which spends the early part of its life on the range eating grass, is 'finished' in the Midwest on grain, which gives it its eating qualities, notably intramuscular fat, the 'marble' (p. 89).

CORN FRITTERS: Kernel corn lightly bound with flour and eggs, shallow fried.

CORN RELISH: A spiced vegetable mixture served with cold meats.

CORN-ON-THE-COB: Ears of corn, freshly gathered, stripped of the husk, boiled in water with milk and sugar for seven minutes. Served with butter.

CORN OYSTERS: Another name for corn fritters.

COTTAGE CHEESE: Many housewives make their own cottage cheese if they have a source of farm milk, otherwise buy it to eat with fried mush, or as a garnish with asparagus, potato salad, canned fruit, dried beef, chicken.

DINGLE DOOS: Folksy expression for hors-d'oeuvre.

DRAFT ROOT BEER: Root beer is an ordinary soft drink which contains some natural flavourings (but not sarsaparilla which was outlawed a few years ago), and foaming agents. Served up with incredible mystique from oaken barrels (which are mere shells for pipes) in frosted mugs as though it was beer. There are stands throughout the Midwest serving it and it is the most popular beverage at drive-ins.

DUTCH LUNCH: Cold cuts, cheese, beer and coffee.

FISH FRY: Although often an event sponsored by church groups, the fish fry is also a restaurant specialty, usually on Fridays, in which as much fried fish as is wanted can be eaten for a *prix fixe*.

FRIED RABBIT: In the well-developed Midwest, rabbits are

the most often taken of small game. Frequently fried, like chicken.

FROGS' LEGS: The states bordering the great lakes, especially Michigan which has a huge lake coast, eat frogs' legs matter of factly, while the rest of the country cannot even abide the idea. These are not the effete little French frogs, but mammoth bulls, with legs fully the size of a chicken's. Often they are like chicken.

FRUIT BUTTERS: Spiced, sugared fruit pulps are frequent mealtime (any meal) garnishings, eaten with bread. Such items, and food like crabapple pickles, add interest to otherwise bland dishes.

GELATINE BELT: A way of describing the Midwest where gelatine as 'aspic' in dessert salads is widely used, perhaps abused.

GOUPE: A thick sauce for ice cream, made with crushed pineapple in syrup, walnuts in syrups or other chopped fruits in syrup.

GRAVY: Gravy is almost always based on the dripping of roasted meat or the fat rendered from fried meat, thickened with flour and developed with water. No spices, except salt and pepper, are used.

GREEN CORN SOUP: Corn is scraped from the cobs of fresh corn, and the cobs boiled to make a broth. The scraped corn is added to the liquid which is then finished with milk and egg yolks.

◆ GROUSE IN WINE SAUCE: Birds marinated in wine with seasonings and then casseroled.

◆ HASHED BROWN POTATOES: Diced cooked potatoes fried in bacon fat and turned out as an omelette.

HOBO SANDWICH: A hot roast beef sandwich on French bread soaked with gravy; quite similar to the English bookmaker's sandwich, served with long greenish hot pepper called a banana pepper.

◆ HOT GREEN SALAD: Spinach and lettuce fried in bacon fat and sprinkled with vinegar.

HOT PEA SALAD: Name for boiled peas and boiled, diced potatoes bound with butter.

HOT POTATO SALAD: Potatoes cooked in their skins, peeled, thinly sliced, seasoned with bacon, onion, vinegar, parsley, sugar, pepper and celery seed.

HOOVER HOG: A folksy way of referring to the armadillo, which, until the depression, during the presidency of Herbert Hoover, was disdained by non-Latin southwesterners.

ICE CREAM SOCIAL: The serving of sweets is common here, where in other areas alcohol would be used. An ice cream social is simply a party at which ice cream and cake are served.

LEMONADE: A favourite summertime beverage made of lemon and sugar, water, and sometimes, for special occasions, egg whites for foam.

LITTLE TURKEYS: Popular 'little turkeys', are pork chops stuffed with a turkey stuffing, e.g. bread stuffing with sausage and onion.

NEAR BEER: Many states having restrictive laws set **a**

maximum on the alcoholic content of beer that can be sold at certain times – to minors, on Sunday, etc. This beer, which is usually below 3·2 alcoholic content by volume, is called near beer.

◆ ORANGE AND CARROT GELATINE SALAD: Grated raw carrot set in a spiced orange jelly.

OLD FASHIONED ICE CREAM: Implies a very wide choice of flavours and a somewhat richer (in eggs) ice cream mixture. Usually the specialty of the ice cream parlour, a replica of the 1920 tea parlour, with wire chairs, marble-topped tables, etc.

◆ OVENFRIED PERCH: Fillets of whole fish coated with butter and crushed cornflakes and potato crisps. Baked in oven.

OVERNIGHT SALAD: A salad left to develop overnight. Made of cherries, pineapples, quarter marshmallows and eggs with whipped cream.

PANCAKES: A thick crêpe, made in many variations: with sourdough (that is, fermented dough), buckwheat flour, buttermilk, blueberries, etc. Eaten for breakfast or a dessert, with molasses, corn syrup or maple syrup.

PASTIES: While these started out as meat pies, they often are made today as meat loaves.

◆ PERSIMMON PUDDING: A chilled mixture of persimmon pulp, walnuts, and crackers.

PHEASANT MULLIGAN: A sort of salmis of pheasant.

PICNIC CHICKENS: In spring and summer, family picnics are accompanied by broiling chickens, split and grilled over the coals with green corn, all the sweeter for being 'borrowed' from some nearby field.

PIE À LA MODE: Refers to a scoop of ice cream served on top of a piece of fruit pie.

PIEPLANT PIE: This little bit of tautology refers to a rhubarb pie. Rhubarb is frequently used along or in combination with berries for pie fillings and sauces.

PITCH IN SUPPERS: Also called covered dish suppers, tureen suppers. A meal to which each of the invited guests contributes a dish. Often held by a local group or a church to raise money. Macaroni and cheese, spinach pie, scalloped potatoes, onions, cole slaw, apple salads and ambrosia are favourite items brought.

POPCORN PUDDING: Popcorn is a special type of corn which when heat-treated will pop up to 30 times the original size. It is a popular snack food when buttered and salted, made into candies and sometimes into pudding by soaking in milk and combining with eggs and cracker crumbs.

PORTERHOUSE: Similar to the T-bone (see MIDWEST) but a much choicer cut in that only two are properly cut from each loin of beef so that the tenderloin muscle is large and prominent.

PRAIRIE OYSTERS: A hangover remedy consisting of an unbroken, raw egg yolk, with Worcestershire sauce, ketchup, vinegar, lemon juice, red pepper sauce, taken from a glass as though it was an oyster.

◆ PRETZELS: Knot-shaped sweet biscuits.

PRIME RIBS OF BEEF: The ribs of beef roasted in the oven, served *au jus*.

◆ **PUMPKIN PIE:** A mixture of cooked pumpkin pulp, egg yolks, cream, sugar, seasonings (called pumpkin pie seasonings, actually cinnamon, nutmeg, mace, clove) combined with whipped egg whites and baked in an unbaked pie shell.

◆ **RABBIT STEW:** A thick stew with vegetables in julienne strips.

ROAST BEEF HASH: A mixture made of the leftover roast beef with onions and potatoes.

ROSIN BAKED POTATO: A 'baked' potato which is more often talked about than eaten. It supposedly had its origin in the turpentine factories of Georgia, when a worker threw a raw potato in a pot of boiling pine rosin. Moments later, the rosin potato popped to the surface, covered with rosin and perfectly cooked on the inside. Although this is a quite excellent way of baking potatoes, it is extremely dangerous because of the inflammability of the rosin. Recently, safe ovens have been designed and are enjoying some use in the West and South.

ROCKY MOUNTAIN TROUT: Local trout usually hatchery-bred. A popular fish item in an area without a seacoast.

SALAD BAR: In many steak restaurants of this area, several cuts of steak are prepared all accompanied by a limited choice of vegetables, usually baked or fried potatoes, and salad and dressing which are taken by the customer in the quantity he wants from a buffet containing a monstrous bowl of salad and sometimes a dozen types of bottled dressing.

SAUCE: Very often in the Midwest, this means a cooked fruit accompaniment to meat, for example, pork with apple sauce.

◆ SCALLOPED TOMATOES: Sliced tomatoes baked with seasonings, butter and bread crumbs.

SHORT ORDERS: Meals that are prepared by the counterman in a restaurant with stools and a counter, rather than tables and chairs. Such foods as ham and eggs, hamburgers and sandwiches are short orders.

SHRIMP COCKTAIL: The most popular hors-d'oeuvre in this area and perhaps in America for a steak meal. Simply boiled, shelled, de-veined, large shrimps with cocktail sauce made of ketchup, chilli sauce, horseradish and seasoning.

SLOPPY JOE'S: A sandwich on a hamburger bun (a round bun of soft bread dough) consisting of sliced or shredded beef, tomato sauce, onion and seasonings.

◆ SMELT SMOKIES: Deep fried smelts, coated in highly seasoned cornmeal mixture.

◆ SMOKED CARP: Carp cut into pieces and smoked over aromatic woods.

SMOTHERED WITH ONIONS: Anything in the Midwest can be covered with fried onions which is called smothering. Most often, steaks and chops are thus suffocated.

SPARERIB PIE: Spareribs chopped into portions, braised and then covered in the braising pan with a biscuit dough.

SWEETBREAD COCKTAIL: Poached sweetbreads, broken into pieces like small oysters and eaten with cocktail sauce (see Shrimp Cocktail).

◆ TAFFY APPLES

T-BONE STEAK: This is what Americans call a sirloin steak. Their sirloin steak is a part of the English steak piece.

TURKEYBONE SOUP: Leftover cooking is an important underground cuisine in America. Turkeybone soup is a way of dealing with leftover Thanksgiving turkey; a broth made of the carcass, garnished with picked meat and thickened with turkey stuffing.

◆ VENISON SOUP: Venison and vegetables simmered slowly.

◆ VINEGAR PIE: A spiced mixture cooked in pastry shell.

◆ WILD RICE: The name of an aquatic grass which grows wild in many areas of the upper Midwest. Although commercial gathering is restricted some Midwesterners gather it themselves for their own use from river banks and swamps.

◆ WILD GOOSE WITH APRICOT STUFFING: Roasted with apple and apricot stuffing.

WILTED SALAD: Once a very popular rural dish in the Midwest. Quite similar to many European treatments of chicory and other bitter greens, made with rendered bacon, bacon fat, and vinegar and served warm.

YALLER BREAD: A folksy way of refering to yellow bread, i.e. corn bread.

YELLOW TURNIPS: Name refers to rutabagas, which are quite popular mashed and candied.

West

The American West has long captured the imagination of small boys and older romantics the world over. It is largely as pictured by John Ford. Cowboys really do live in bunkhouses, they do ride in rodeos, they do go on round-ups, they do carry guns to shoot varmints. Much has changed in the West, cowboys are better paid, bunkhouses are often modern dormitories, the helicopter and jeep coexist with the horse, but the substance is still here, because the cattle are still here, the hills are still here and the sun is still here.

Sparse pasturage and sparse water mean that ranch houses are far apart. The land only supports a very small population at a very low population density. The nearest neighbour may be thirty miles from the ranch house, the nearest town a hundred miles. A town is defined as a gas pump, a grocery store (called the general store) and a post office sub-station.

In the summer, housewives may get into town to 'trade' once a week, in the winter; blizzards and huge drifts may mean months between shopping trips. The emphasis in cooking in the West is on self-reliance. Store-bought items are few: baking powder, bacon, salt pork, evaporated milk, some canned vegetables, cornmeal, dried fruit, flour, gelatine, coffee, ketchup, table syrup, molasses, potatoes, sugar, salt, rice, pepper and vinegar, compared with the literally thousands of items which enter other American homes. Fresh meat comes from game and home butchering of whatever the ranchers raise. Beef and lamb are common, pork is not.

The housewife may gather berries and wild vegetables in season, but the land does not support much wild vegetation, and the cattle generally consume what there is. Kitchen gardens for greens are common but not extensive.

People in this part of the country prefer meat and starch, and rely often on dried fruit for bulk. Much of the time, the men of the household and the ranch hands for whom the housewife must cook, are occupied out on the range, and cook for themselves for long periods. They use the omnipresent dutch oven as an all-round cooking vessel.

These ovens are made of heavy cast iron in various capacities. All resemble a bucket. They distribute the heat evenly and hold it efficiently. They have a snug concave cover so that coals can be put in the top for baking.

A dutch oven, a coffee pot, a sack filled with premixed biscuit ingredients, a piece of salt and a water container are considered adequate basics for a week or two of outdoor living.

Elaborate ranching operations have a permanent cook and chuckwagon, which these days is usually a four-wheel drive truck, as a mobile kitchen.

Most of the time the chuckwagon cook only offers the familiar biscuits, meat and beans. His only unique contribution may be some kind of pie (apple, cherry, prune, venison, or green tomato), which causes the chuckwagon to be called the 'pie box' as well.

Biscuits are a thing of pride, and most cowboys are quite vocal in their criticisms of other people's biscuits. They used to be made of sourdough, but today baking powder is much more common.

Housewives also pride themselves on their baked goods. Home-made bread makes frequent appearances. Home-made preserves and home-canned goods are entered in county fairs to compete for blue ribbons. In many areas, the county fair and the rodeo are the prime social occasions of the year, the one time when the people can get out of themselves and show off their skills.

In the highly urbanized, industrialized United States, it becomes harder and harder to keep young people on the ranch. Life is tough, although there is plenty to eat and enough money for simple luxuries. Many of the people in the West opened their land themselves and view the comparative prosperity of today as the just reward for their years of effort. The younger people are hard put to see beyond the endless chores, and the city has a siren's call. The simple life, they find, is plain.

BAKED IDAHO POTATOES: The baked Idaho has long been the traditional accompaniment to steaks. It has been made simply by rubbing the potato with fat or butter, and baking it in the oven, splitting the baked potato then garnishing with a variety of toppings including sour cream and chives, and Parmesan cheese. Most often it is eaten simply with butter.

Today the use of metal foil as an envelope is quite common. The product is rather different as the potato is steamed rather than baked. The foil goes to the table.

♦ BARBECUED BEEF SHORTRIBS: Ribs cut into small sections and coated with barbecue sauce and baked.

♦ BEAN SOUP: White beans and vegetables simmered with ham bone.

♦ BEEF BRAINS WITH EGGS: Brains chopped and fried in butter with eggs. Served on toast.

♦ BRAISED ANTELOPE: Game of all kinds makes a considerable contribution to meals in the West, indeed elk, deer, moose may account for as much as one-third of the meat eaten in some areas.

◆ BRAISED OXTAIL: Braised with root vegetables, onions, tomatoes. Powdered cloves in the seasoning.

BRIGHAM TEA: An infusion made from any of a variety of local shrubs by the Mormons of Utah. (Named after their founder Brigham Young who had forbidden genuine coffee and tea.)

◆ BROILED RAINBOW TROUT: Coated with savoury butter and grilled.

BUCK STEW: A simple stew of venison with diced onions and carrots. Generally eaten from August to November when the bucks are at their prime. The does are best supposedly from November to January.

BUCKAROO BEANS: Another version of baked beans with garlic, onion, slab pork, chilli powder, mustard, oregano.

BUFFALO BERRY JELLY: A rich garnet-coloured jelly made from the local buffalo berry which has an almost ideal proportion of pectin and acid, giving a very delicate gel.

BURNT LEATHER CAKE: A butter cake iced with caramel syrup, which is a very popular confection in the west.

CANNED COW: Folksy way of referring to evaporated milk, which is a common ranch supply.

CHICKEN FRIED STEAKS: 'Chicken frying' indicates treating any meat as though it were fried chicken, that is, with a breading or a batter.

◆ CORNED VENISON: Pickled in a sweet brine.

COWBOY BISCUITS: A simple biscuit formula made traditionally by cowboys mixing the dough right in the flour sack by feel. Covered with bacon grease, they were baked in a dutch oven, the cowboys' all-purpose cooking vessel.

◆ COWBOY BEANS: Red beans simmered with bacon, chilli sauce and corn syrup. Used as part of chuckwagon dinner.

CUSH: Stale corn bread mixed with butter and hot water to form a croquette which is fried for breakfast.

◆ DEVILLED LAMB RIBS: Simmered in a spiced sauce.

FLANNEL CAKES: Pancakes. An expression favoured in the west.

FLAPJACKS: Pancakes.

FLAT CARS: Another name for pancakes.

FRIED COOT: A frequent treatment of the coot.

HAYMAKERS BREAKFAST: A steak with French fried onions, fried potatoes, biscuits, pressed pies, fruit and honey.

HOT ROCKS: Name given to biscuits made in the outdoors on a round-up.

JAVA: A folksy word for coffee.

JERKY: Refers to any dried meat (beef or game) cut in strips, salted and dried – usually sun dried – as a means of preservation.

KOLACES: These are Czechoslovakian tarts filled with jam. A large Czech population makes this middle European food familiar to many Westerners.

LICK: Folksy way of referring to table syrup, which is used on many dishes including meats.

◆ MOLASSES WHEAT BREAD

MORMON BREAD: A bread made from the roots of the ego lily, part of the sub-cuisine of the Mormon religious sect centred in Utah.

MOUNTAIN OYSTERS: Offals are extremely popular in this section of the country. Much lamb hearts, kidneys, etc., are eaten. So are lamb fry, euphemistically called mountain oysters. People have learned to eat offals quickly before rigor which toughens them sets in.

MULLIGANS: Mulligans are simple stews of whatever is available: venison, moose, beef, pheasant. Associated with masculine cooking, campfires, and hobo jungles (encampments of vagabonds).

PINCH OFF: Name given to biscuits generally, but actually refers to old-time practice of mixing biscuit ingredients in the sack of flour and pinching off dough to bake in a dutch oven.

RASPBERRY VINEGAR: A sourish drink of raspberries infused in vinegar, something like lemonade, taken by the Mormons, who are forbidden coffee and tea.

RHUBARB WINE: A folk wine made from pie plants (p.75). Beets and varieties of berries are also treated this way.

RODEO ROAST: Actually a way of referring to the barbecue (see Southwest) which is part of the frequent rodeos.

SAGEBRUSH HONEY: One of the local honeys made from one of the few plants that can grow in the arid parts of the West.

SMORGASBORD: A style of dining, Scandinavian in origin, in which diners prepare their own plates from a choice of dishes on a central table. In this region the word is used more legitimately than it often is elsewhere: cold fish, vegetables, salads, cold meats, etc.

♦ SMOTHERED PHEASANT: Simmered with cream.

SOURDOUGH: Originally a leavening made of wild yeasts, somewhat sophisticated by preparing a special leavening dough called a sponge of dry yeast. Sourdough baked goods, doughnuts, breads and pancakes, are familiar in the West.

STACK OF WHEATS: A pile of pancakes.

♦ SUNSHINE COLE SLAW: Cabbage, carrots and peppers, shredded, tossed in mayonnaise.

♦ VENISON MINCEMEAT: A sweet mixture of minced venison, suet, apples, dried fruits and spices, used in pies.

♦ WILD RICE: A wild grain with a nutty flavour, rather expensive.

Southwest

The Southwest has a long culinary memory. Most of the people called Anglos, to differentiate them from Mexican Americans, came from other regions. The Southwest was an area of secondary or tertiary settlement. Pioneer families moved from the East Coast to the Southwest or, in many cases, from the East to the Midwest to the Southwest. They brought with them a great many regional dishes which had a personal validity for them. They encountered regional cuisine similar in all respects to the Mexican cuisines of the northern provinces. Spanish exploration of the area and influence had begun before the colonization of Jamestown. For many years, New Orleans, which is on the eastern periphery of this area, and connected by the Mississippi and the Ohio Rivers to the East, was the jumping off point of the Anglo-American colonizers. They brought with them an affection for French food that is still evident in some regional dishes.

Along the border with Mexico were included many split towns. There has also been the presence of migratory Mexican farm workers. Both these factors have kept the Spanish influence completely alive.

Indian culture is as viable in the Southwest as anywhere in the country. Indian dishes preserved within the matrix of Mexican cuisine have survived here after a fashion.

Two major industries, cattle raising and citrus fruit cultivation, make major contributions to the cuisine.

The barbecue as such has antecedents in the earliest human settlements of the area. There are several interesting variations: the pit barbecue, the oven barbecue, the open grate barbecue. The pit barbecue, also called ground cookery, is quite possibly the oldest form. The original Indians would carry a fire inside their round adobe houses and lay it on a pit in the centre. The smoke drifted upwards, hopefully, through the opening in the wall. It was a long time before houses became square and a proper fireplace against the wall of the house evolved. Because of the inconvenience of the smoke, a lot of cooking was done out of doors in a beehive oven of the type still used in the Argentines. That is, clay ovens which are heated, stuffed with wrapped parcels of meat and seasonings, closed and allowed to slowly cook. In the modern pit barbecue, the same effect is encouraged.

First a pit is dug about four by six feet, and lined with black malapi rock. A fire is burned in the hole or raked in and allowed to heat it. Then about 200 pounds of meat are cut in even pieces of five or six pounds and either put in a tub with seasonings or wrapped with the seasonings in cheese cloth. The next step in the tub method is to close the tub and bury it on the coals, packing the whole pit with dirt and stones. In the cheese-cloth method, tin sheets are layered on the coals, then several layers of burlap. The cheese-cloth bags are covered with water-soaked burlap and tied with bailing wire, placed between metal sheets, covered with hot rocks and a fire racked on top. Then the whole mound is covered with a trap, dirt and stones. The cooking process may take 12 hours.

The hot sauce that has become identified with the barbecue is either eaten with the meat or in some cases rubbed on it. It might be remarked that the meat is not roasted by this process but wet baked.

The open grate barbecue is a form of charcoal broiling in which the meat is cooked over coals, swabbed with a basting sauce and eaten with spicy sauces. Oven barbecue is reserved for large cuts, which are roasted, while being basted several times with sauce.

Most of the time, pit barbecues, which are extremely complex, involving twelve hours of preparation time, are community events, part of a 'shindig' as feasts are called in this area. There are special barbecue masters, who can, on one occasion, prepare enough food for 6,000 people. The other barbecue forms are by way of an extension of this process to make it more convenient.

Barbecue is also a popular restaurant item. In many instances, however, the only thing the restaurant barbecue has in common with a real barbecue is a ketchup-based sauce.

Mexican food in the non-Mexican restaurant suffers the same sort of fate. In the Mexican quarters of the Southwest, it is virtually indistinguishable from the peasant Mexican food south of the border. In restaurants, diners and drive-ins, it is generally less spicy and may in fact be bought from commercial packing plants.

The American Southwest has become synonymous the world over with beef cattle production. While this area produces much of the beef cattle, every state of the union has some cattle production. California has a cattle population equal to that of Oklahoma; even Florida, Georgia, Kentucky and Tennessee are considerable cattle producers.

Beef, of course, dominates the agriculture of the Southwest; beef is king in these states. As the United States does not have native *Bos* species, the varieties that are raised in the United States were imported or carefully crossbred. Because of the preference of Americans for beef and their willingness to pay for premium beef, cattle raisers have a veritable carte blanche in developing and producing the finest beef cattle in the world. Most of the initial development work on beef cattle breeds was started in the middle of the eighteenth century.

The important beef breeds in the United States originated in Great Britain, primarily as the result of the great British breeders, Robert Bakewell, the Collings brothers, Richard Tomkins and Hugh Watson. During the latter part of the eighteenth century, the United States began importing representative samples of the principal beef cattle breeds: Aberdeen Angus, Devon, Galloway, Hereford, Red Poll, Highland, Shorthorn and Sussex. All these breeds were successfully introduced to the United States. In general these beef breeds can be distinguished from other types of cattle by their true beef form and marked fleshing qualities.

Several dual purpose breeds were developed to produce a higher level of milk and butterfat.

Work is constantly going on to improve the eating qualities of American beef. Breeders are using such sophisticated techniques as radioisotope potassium tracing and sonic waves to determine proportions of fat and lean in breeding bulls, in their efforts to produce the particularly block animal that has become identified with American beef.

Although the cattle are raised in the grazing lands of the Southwest, the prime and choice beef, the two topmost American grades, are usually finished in the Midwest's feeder pens to produce the intramuscular fat, the 'marble', that connoisseur's prize. Although there has been some controversy in Europe, objectively one must say marbled beef is more tender and more juicy.

ADOBO: Name given to the barbecue sauce of chillies, garlic, wild marjoram, vinegar and bread crumbs with which a fowl was dredged.

AGUACATE: The wild avocado which is much smaller and less meaty than the domestic and hybridized varieties. Still available in Southwestern towns and in northern Mexico.

ASAFRÁN: A wild saffron type, used in making yellow rice.

BARBECUE: A meal with a main course of meat cooked by the barbecue method (see text above) with cowboy beans, coleslaw, potato salad, sliced tomatoes and onion salad, pickles, apple pie and coffee.

◆ BARBECUED RABBIT: Joints boned and then cooked in oven with barbecue sauce.

BARBECUED ARMADILLO: One of the few uses in America of a reptile as a gourmet meal. The armadillo and armoured lizard, once removed from the shell and scrupulously cleaned of fat and sweat glands, resembles pork flesh.

◆ BAR-B-CUE SAUCE: Ketchup, mustard, Worcestershire sauce, horseradish, brown sugar, chilli pepper, cumin, spices (dill, bay, thyme, red pepper, etc.), onion and garlic.

BATTER FRIED SQUASH BLOSSOM: A familiar European treatment for blossoms, shared with the Zuni Indians of the Southwest. Essentially, the same as treatments for acacia blossoms, etc.

BEAN SAUCE: Used for dipping flat pancakes called tortillas. Made of red pinto beans, garlic, cumin, bacon, chilli powder and salso picante (Mexican hot sauce).

BLUE CORNMEAL: A type of cornmeal ground from calico corn, that is, corn with different coloured kernels in the same cob.

CACTUS SALAD: An occasional dish in the Southwest where cactus is available; quite simply drained, canned tender shoots of cactus in oil and vinegar dressing.

CAILLETTE: Cabbage stuffed with bread crumbs, eggs and seasonings.

CALICO BISCUITS: Biscuits with finely chopped green and red (sweet) pepper within.

♦ CARNE ADOBADA: Pork chops in a hot chilli sauce.

CARNE TATEMADA: Spanish expression still in use for barbecued beef.

♦ CHILLI: While obviously of Southwestern origin, the originators of this spice dish would have trouble recognizing it in the chilli parlours around the Midwest because it contains no herbs, little seasoning and a lot of tomato sauce. There are places where you can get chilli 'a hundred ways', with rice, macaroni (called chilli mac), etc.

CHILLI ANCHOS: Wide (ancho) chilli peppers used to make chilli pastes for seasoning. They are available dried: fat, wrinkled-looking, reddish black in colour.

♦ CHILLI COLORADO CON TORTITAS DE HUEVO: Spoonfuls of egg mixture. Fried and served in a chilli sauce with fried fish.

♦ CHILLI CON CARNE: A stew of kidney or pinto beans with onions, chopped beef, garlic, oregano, cumin and chilli powder.

♦ CHILES RELLENOS: Peppers stuffed with minced pork and deep fried.

CHILLI MOLE: A dish prepared of ground beef and pork with chilli powder, garlic, vinegar, and ground bitter chocolate as seasoning.

CHILLITIPINES: Small, round chilli peppers.

CHORIZO: The country sausage which, in all respects, resembles the Spanish prototype.

CHUCKWAGON DINNER: Restaurant meals supposedly in the style of the old west. Usually means some sort of barbecued beef and beans.

◆ COLACHE: A stew of squash, corn and tomatoes.

◆ ENCHILADAS: Tortillas filled with meat mixture and baked with cheese, onions and chilli sauce.

EJOTES: Green beans cooked in oil with chillies, chicas and peppers.

◆ FRIJOLES: The Spanish word for beans but refers, specifically in this area, to the pink bean which is water-cooked in large quantities and then fried (refritos) for several meals.

GARBANZOS: Chick peas, popular here as they are wherever Spanish populations exist.

GUAVA: Fruit served in chutneys, jellies and desserts.

JALAPEÑOS: A variety of chilli.

JAVELINA HAM: A wild boar-type animal in the Southwest which is treated like pig, but is in fact quite a different animal, with small hams and large meaty forelegs.

MAGUEY: Mexican aloe used to make various fermented liquids: pulque, which is a fermented drink; tequila, which is a white alcohol; and mescal, which is somewhere in between.

MANGOES: Here refers to a sweet green pepper used as a

pickle, not to be mistaken with the tropical fruit usually made into chutney.

MANO: The stone pestle used with a metate.

MASA: Corn dehulled by lime treatment then ground in small quantities in a metate with a mano – rectangular, light, concave stone and a stone pestle for making tortillas, etc.

METATE: The concave stone used to grind corn into meal.

MOLACEJETE Y TEJOLOTE: Mortar and pestle, of Aztec origin, similar in all respects to other stone mortar and pestle except the mortar stands on three little legs.

NATILLAS: A sort of boiled custard pudding.

NOPAL, NOPALITOS: A type of cactus, prepared in cans and hence widely used.

OREGANO: Wild marjoram.

PANOCHA: A dessert-like Indian pudding eaten in Southeastern Spanish-American homes on Ash Wednesday.

PEPITAS: Squash seeds soaked in water, hulled and then toasted.

PESHOFA: Cracked, dry, shelled corn, ground in a mortar and pestle, fermented, dried in the sun and combined with beef in a sort of stew.

PICHOLA: Pork, tomatoes, chopped onion, chilli sauce and hominy all combined in a sort of long-cooked stew.

PIÑON: A purée of pine nuts, with a little water, dropped and cooked on a griddle.

PIÑON SOUP: A pine nut soup, developed as a chicken velouté, with a purée of pine nuts, seasoned with coriander and mint.

◆ POLLO GUISADO: Jointed chicken simmered with tomatoes, green chilli and mushrooms.

POZOLE FRIJOLES Y MAIZ: Translates as beans and hominy, a very old dish still enjoyed in the Southwest.

PUCHITAS: A cake made with baking powder and flavoured with anise.

◆ PURSLANE SALAD: A salading with thick succulent leaves.

RANCHO SAGE: Diced salt pork, onion, garlic, tomatoes, etc., served with fried eggs.

RED BEANS AND RICE: Red kidney beans, salt pork or ham hock, onion cooked until a sauce is produced, seasoned with thyme, sage and red pepper. Served over rice.

RED EYE: The local name for cheap whisky. Also called rotgut.

SALSA DE CHILE TOSTADO: A red purée of toasted chilli peppers, onions, olive oil, used as a sauce and a 'dip'.

SASSAFRAS TEA: A favourite infusion brewed from the bark of the sassafras after the sap has risen in spring.

◆ SMOTHERED WILD DUCK: Jointed pieces browned and simmered gently in milk.

SON OF A GUN STEW: A variety of meat stew of calf's offal simply water-cooked with a little garlic. The choice morsel is the 'marrow gut', the tube connecting the stomachs of milk-feeding calves, filled with partially digested milk.

SOPA CAPIROTADA: A dessert made like bread pudding containing piñon nuts, cheese and sugar.

SOPA DE ALBONDIGAS: Meatball soups made with pork and beef meatballs highly seasoned with chilli pepper and garlic.

◆ ROAST TURKEY WITH BARBECUE SAUCE: Stuffed with celery leaves and onion, basted with barbecue sauce.

◆ TAMALE LOAF: A spiced meat loaf, made with minced meat, corn, green olives and spices.

SOPAIPILLA: A hot dough product sometimes like a dough, other times like a popover. Sometimes called 'sofa pillow' from the Spanish name and its appearance.

◆ SQUAW BREAD: A simple baking powder leavened bread, fried instead of baked in a heavy skillet.

◆ TACOS: Fried tortillas.

TAMALE PIE: A casserole dish made of ground meat between two layers of cornmeal seasoned with chilli.

TAMALES: Corn husk filled with a mixture of pork, chicken, seasonings, and cornmeal, and poached. Only the filling is eaten.

TOMATES FRESCADILLAS: The wild original tomato still growing in some parts of the Southwest and Mexico. About the size of a damson plum with a thickish skin and a greenish purple colour.

◆ TORTILLAS: A pancake made of biscuit dough, or more usually of cornmeal.

◆ TOSTADOS: Tacos stuffed.

VIBORA DE CASCABEL: The local name of rattlesnake, which is sometimes, but very rarely, eaten, largely because of reluctance to eat reptile and the difficulties of capture. Sometimes fried like chicken, other times barbecued.

VENISON CHILLI: Minced venison cooked with red beans.

◆ VENISON SAUSAGE: Minced venison and pork, made into patties and frozen until needed.

Farwest

This is the land of the ostrich egg omelette, and the barbecue for sixty thousand people. There is more, it's bigger, it's juicier, it's sweeter and it's prettier in the American West: California, Washington and Oregon.

The sea and streams are prodigal: rainbow trout, shad, langouste, crabs, oysters, shrimp, bass, albacore, smelts, dabs, and salmon abound.

The valleys are fecund; kale, shallots, Chinese cabbage, okra, pimentos, field peas, watercress, cranberries, mangoes, pineapples, guavas, youngberries, dewberries, and more than a few vineyards.

The orchards and groves are extravagant: limes, quinces, tangelos, pecans, filberts, walnuts, chestnuts, kumquats, figs, dates, pomegranate, persimmons, avocados, jujubes (Chinese dates), loquats (Japanese medlar), grandilla (passion fruit), and papayas.

The slopes and woods are generous mountain sheep and goats, wild boar, rabbits, quail, sage hens, wild duck, geese, turkey, pheasant, partridge, bear, deer, elk, grouse, prairie hens and snow geese.

All this bounty has encouraged the most capricious invention. Most of the bizarre culinary creations with which America is credited originated in the Farwest. California can claim an extraordinary reconciliation of Chinese, Mexican, Italian, American Indian, French and Japanese cookery.

Meals in the Farwest borrow from all these traditions and

make use of their wide variety of produce. Soups are a good example. The clam chowder of New England is made in the Farwest with abalone or pismo clams. Puchero, Sopa à la Espagnola, Gazpacho – all profit from the splendid local vegetables. French crab or shrimp bisques with local crustaceans, or German cherry soup with native cherries are likely to figure on menus.

A first course of salad is frequently served rather than soup – especially in restaurants. The tendency at home is to have three-course menus: entrée, salad and dessert.

In any case, these salads are composed of fruits, seafood and seasonable vegetables in combinations that make a strong visual statement. Creamy green avocados, purple plums, black olives, pink and white crab meat and white cottage cheese figure in a variety of floral arrangements.

Even simple salads, of oak leaf lettuce (bronze fringed), chicory, endive, escarole and romaine, are dressed with colourful sauces and garnished with bits of olives, red onions, or strips of pimentos.

Seafood salads for first course or main dishes feature either crab meat, langouste or tuna fish. Other fish are reserved for main courses. A fish course as such is a rarity.

Although there is a strong Italian influence on fish cookery, most Farwesterners simply broil fish, with a generous sprinkling of lemon or lime juice. Tuna is sometimes roasted like veal. Broiled salmon steaks, broiled or boiled crustaceans, fried abalone 'steaks', baked trout, broiled halibut . . . these figure in the average repertoire.

Popular dishes like lobster Cantonese, moules marinières, and fish stews, are left to restaurants.

The emphasis on broiled food is carried over to entrées. Much meat is broiled, frequently out-of-doors on a charcoal-fired grill. A year-round splendid climate encourages this kind of cooking.

Seasoning tends to herbal blends or to tomato ketchup

basting sauces. Considerable emphasis is put on the charcoal itself. Some cooks burn the wood to make their own coals. Others burn a small herb bunch or a fragrant resinous wood on the coals just for flavour, or baste the grilling meat with a whisk made from a herb bunch.

Although the popular term for outdoor cooking is to bar-b-cue, the word really refers to a very specific process, which is seldom attempted in the home.

A pit must be dug, then a fire is burned in it for twelve hours to create a bed of hot coals. Next a sheet of galvanized iron is placed over the coals and covered with wet sacking. Then twenty-pound chunks of meat, painted with sauce and wrapped in a sauce-soaked cheese cloth, are placed in the pit. More sacks cover the meat, and then a roof of galvanized iron, stones and sand is constructed to keep the heat in. Fourteen hours later, the meat is cooked. The universal use of bar-b-cue sauce (generally ketchup based and highly spiced) has given the name to other outdoor cooking.

Out-of-doors and in, vegetables are often cooked with the entrée. Half grapefruits are broiled with meats, reflecting a general preference for fruit relishes with meat. Tomatoes have their place on the outdoor grill. Corn-on-the-cob, after a soaking in salt water, is often grilled in the husks (the silk having been removed), on the coals, while potatoes wrapped in metal foil roast in a corner.

As the Farwest especially is a major producer of almost every vegetable, menus follow seasonal crops. Vegetables which have limited use elsewhere are common there: artichokes, brussel sprouts, asparagus, Chinese peas, leeks and water chestnuts are good examples.

Short round local rice is favoured, over the more widely used long grain. Frequently it is toasted in a heavy pan, before being steam-cooked or cooked by the pilaf method. Polenta, which makes a very rare appearance nationally, has a place among the Farwesterners' food.

While all breads are popular, especially fruit breads and yeast muffins, most Farwesterners favour 'garlic' bread. Several cloves of garlic are mixed with a half pound of softened butter for half an hour and then removed. A loaf of sourdough French bread is split lengthwise, buttered, re-formed and left to absorb the garlic taste. Sometimes it is sprinkled with Parmesan cheese, or a spice such as oregano, basil or thyme. The prepared bread is toasted in a paper bag in a hot oven for ten minutes.

Farwesterners of Mexican origin generally eat tortillas of dried corn (masa) or flour instead of bread. Once these pancakes were made by women who slapped them on their bare thighs until they were paper-thin. Today modern factories produce this staple food, although not to the standards of the thigh slappers.

Almost every Farwestern family, regardless of national origin, eats a Mexican meal once a week . . . usually, enchiladas, frijoles, refritos, chilli or tamales. These products are available in numerous inexpensive restaurants throughout the Farwest and also can be bought frozen in formed aluminium foil trays for home preparation.

Desserts in the Farwest tend to feature fruits, sometimes canned, frozen or home-stewed, but largely fresh. Berry pies, date breads, figs in wine, chocolate cakes, strawberry short-cakes, orange and walnut tortes are often featured. A creamy semi-soft cheese, Monterey Jack, is most appreciated with fruit as a dessert.

ABALONE STEAK: The most common method of preparing abalone (a large shellfish) is to cut the muscle or foot into $\frac{1}{3}$-inch slices and pound with a meat hammer, dip in egg and fine bread crumbs and fry for a few seconds.

◆ APPLESAUCE CAKE: A moist spiced cake incorporating apple sauce, walnuts, raisins.

ASPIC: Aspic (pronounced aspeek in America), although an important part of French cuisine for centuries, has become the keynote of many American menus as moulds, salads and desserts. Tomato aspic is extremely popular

◆ AVOCADO MOULDED SALAD: Avocado mousse set with gelatine, chilled and served with lettuce and avocado slices.

BILLY GOATS: A type of cookie, seasoned with cinnamon, cloves and filled with dates and walnut meats.

BURRITO: Name given to a pancake mixture filled with ground meat seasoned with chilli. Reputedly made first by Father Juan Crespi who started European wheat growth in the Los Angeles, California, area.

◆ BARBECUED HALIBUT STEAKS: Halibut marinated in barbecue sauce and grilled.

CARPETBAG STEAK: A tenderloin steak that has been stuffed with sautéed oysters, then grilled.

CHICKEN IN THE BASKET: Actually fried chicken in napkins and served on a bed of French fries in a wicker basket. Eaten with the fingers. Part of drive-in fare.

◆ CLAM SOUFFLÉ: Minced clams mixed with eggs, crackers, onion, etc., and baked.

CHICKEN OF THE SEA: Another name for tuna fish.

OREGON TART: A rich latticed flan with cranberries, similar to a mid-European torte.

CHRISTMAS TART: An open tart with a lattice top containing a filling of butter, filberts, cranberries and orange juice.

CIOPPINO: A California dish of Portuguese inspiration which is in all respects a bouillabaisse of native fish lacking saffron, but with peppers and white wine.

COFFIN SALADS: A folksy way of referring to salads in large wooden bowls.

CRAB FINGERS: Crab's legs dipped in beaten eggs and then cracker crumbs, fried in butter.

CRAB'S LEGS PALACE COURT: A recipe from that famous hotel destroyed in the San Francisco fire. An artichoke filled with what Europeans called salade russe, with five or six crab's legs on top, covered with Thousand Island dressing.

CRAB LOUIS: Actually a sauce for cold crab. Made of mayonnaise, heavy cream, chilli sauce, chopped green pepper, green onion, green olives, and lemon juice.

♦ CRABURGERS: The Farwest abounds with drive-in restaurants. A whole subcuisine of items that can be eaten out of hand and prepared ahead has been developed. The ubiquitous hamburger has had numerous spin-offs, among these are the craburger, a crab salad on the familiar bun; and the pizza burger, a meat patty with mozzarella cheese, tomato sauce and oregano.

CRACKED CRAB: Small crabs simply boiled in salted water and eaten from the shell. An extremely popular dish hot and cold.

DIPS: Small solid mixtures of various foods and seasoning in a cheese or sour cream base, scooped on raw vegetables, potato chips or other extended cereal products (corn chips, pizza-flavoured chips, etc.) eaten with cocktails.

◆ SALMON SOUR CREAM DIP: Salmon blended with pepper sauce and sour cream, garnished with caviar.

DOUGH GODS: Pieces of yeast dough fried in deep fat.

FLOAT: The combination of ice cream and soda pop in the same glass.

FRIED CREAM: An interesting dish of cream thickened with cornstarch (cornflour) and egg yolks into a custard, turned out on a board, cut oblong, dipped in egg and salted cracker crumbs, then deep fried and set ablaze with rum.

FRIED RAZOR CLAMS: Clams dipped in egg batter and deep fried.

FRUIT COCKTAIL: The Farwest, especially California, makes considerable use of fresh fruit macedoine as an hors-d'oeuvre.

GRUNIONS: Small fish-like sliversides which come up to the beach to lay their eggs and are gathered in California in season as a sort of sport; deep fried like smelt.

GUACAMOLE: A dish of definite Mexican origin. A purée of avocado, garlic, and tomato with spicy seasonings.

◆ HANGTOWN FRY: A dish that is said to have been developed in Parker's Exchange, a saloon in San Francisco, California, in 1853. Made of oysters, ham and eggs.

STUFFED KING CRAB LEGS: Stuffed with mushrooms, crabmeat and grated cheese.

MCGINTIES: A sort of apple pie of dried apples cut in squares.

MONTE CRISCO: A popular sandwich of sliced turkey, Swiss

or Cheddar cheese, made in three layers, dipped in egg and milk and fried in butter.

OLYMPIA PEPPER ROAST: Olympia oysters cooked in a barbecue sauce.

OYSTERS KIRKPATRICK: A Palace Court recipe. Oysters in the shell covered with ketchup, bacon and oven-baked.

PALACE HOTEL DRESSING: A popular mayonnaise dressing based on San Francisco hotel recipes. Contains anchovy fillet, garlic, onion, mayonnaise, heavy cream, lemon juice and parsley.

PEANUT BUTTER LOAF: One of the many baking adventures of California; dates, figs, oranges, etc., in a bread recipe.

PEAR SALAD: Bartlett pears, cottage cheese or cream cheese, maraschino, with romaine lettuce and mayonnaise with cream.

QUESADILLA: Small cheese turnovers made of tortilla.

◆ RHUBARB SHERBERT: Cooked rhubarb, cream, eggs blended and frozen.

SAMBOBURGERS: (See Craburgers).

SEVEN-UP SALAD: One of the many uses of gelatine and salad vegetables. Combine gelatine, salad vegetables, apple sauce and a bottled soft drink – Seven-Up.

SHAKE: A milk and ice cream beverage with flavouring, combined by special high-speed whipping to give a thick homogeneous liquid, sometimes so thick it must be eaten with a spoon.

WESTERN SANDWICH: An omelette made with chopped ham, green peppers, onion and eaten between slices of bread.

WINE SALAD DRESSING: Red wine, oil and seasonings.

Minor Cuisines

HAWAIIAN

The state of Hawaii, actually eight volcanic islands, is the only part of the United States not on the North American continent. It is $4\frac{1}{2}$ hours by jet from the Pacific Coast, which has allowed it to maintain a unique cosmopolitan culture, and substantially kept Hawaiian cuisine from influences of American foodways from other areas. The only exception is California where some attention is paid to Hawaiian and Polynesian cookery.

Most racial groups of the Far East are represented in the Islands' population of 600,000. Chinese, Japanese, Filipino, Korean, European (including Anglo-Saxon and a strong Portuguese and Spanish tradition) dominate the native Hawaiian cookery which is primarily represented by the Luau.

At an authentic Luau, the featured meat dish is a pig that has been cooked in an underground oven called an *imu*. The salad is Lomi Lomi Salmon, a mixture of salted or smoked salmon, tomatoes, green onion and lemon juice. Chicken Luau is a combination of chicken and taro leaves cooked in coconut milk and baked or broiled sweet potatoes (or breadfruit) are served as vegetables. *Poi* (taro root pounded into a paste) might be considered the rice or potatoes of the Islands and is probably the most discussed dish of a Luau table. It is a staple food that the Hawaiians use not only with Luaus but eat plain or with milk and sugar as cereal. It has a strange mild flavour and texture. It is seldom eaten by outsiders although they taste it and talk about it almost without exception.

As an authentic Luau is a considerable undertaking, even in the Islands, the spirit rather than the detail influences Hawaiian-style meals, as is reflected in the following recipes. Rather than a whole pig, a pork loin is used as the main meat. Barbecued spareribs in a sweet and sour marinade is typical of modern Hawaiian cuisine. Baked yams with pineapple substitute for breadfruit; rice takes the place of *poi*. Spinach rather than taro leaves are used, etc.

Hawaii is one of the most prosperous states in the union. Its income per family is rather high, unemployment is well below the national level. Some of these advantages are offset by the generally high cost of living since many products, including food, must be imported from the mainland.

The Islands' main crops are sugar and pineapple. Only recently has rum manufacture become an industry. A fine delicate rum with a dry taste and fine bouquet is being produced.

Macadamia nuts are a minor crop of increasing importance and considerable gastronomic interest. Hawaii is the only state in the union that grows coffee called Kona, which has a full body and very fine aroma. The Islands also export passion fruit (likikoi) juice, and guava nectar to the mainland.

A variety of vegetables as well as taro, mangoes, avocados, bean sprouts, papayas, guavas, pohas, green mangoes, swamp cabbage and citrus fruits are grown for the Islands' own consumption. Beef of quality is raised on the Islands themselves, although some is imported.

The affluence of the natives, a considerable tourist industry, and the cosmopolitan population, make possible some splendid restaurants and hotel dining rooms featuring authentic Pacific Island food, Japanese tea houses, the more obscure schools of Chinese cooking, Korean, Tahitian and

Filipino cuisine, as well as some French and Italian establishments.

◆ BUL KOGI: Sirloin marinated in soy sauce mixture and grilled.

◆ BUTTERFLY SHRIMP ALOHA NUI LOAH: Shrimps split down the back but not through the tail, dipped in batter and deep fat fried to resemble butterflies.

◆ CHICKEN WITH LUAU: Stew of chicken with a spinach-like plant.

◆ DIAMOND HEAD DUCK: Duck stuffed with whole orange, marinated with rum, roasted with honey, orange and rum.

GRILLED HAM LEILANI: Ham with pineapple and barbecue sauce.

◆ HAUPIA: A coconut pudding.

HALAKAHIKI (PINEAPPLE LUAU STYLE): Standing pineapples which appear whole and uncut but which are hollowed, cored, cut into long spears and reassembled with the top as a lid – one of the desserts of the Hawaiian Luau.

◆ LAULAU: Pork cooked with salt fish in Luau leaves and steamed.

◆ LOMI LOMI SALMON: Lomi Lomi means kneaded or massaged in Hawaiian. Lomi Lomi Salmon is King Salmon kneaded with the fingers to remove the bones, then chopped, mixed with fresh tomatoes and green onions and served ice cold.

◆ PINEAPPLE MENEHUNE: Fresh pineapple with egg, rum and butter sauce.

PUAA KALUA (BAKED PORK): Whole pig cooked in the underground oven or 'imu'. The 'imu' is Polynesia's original pressure cooker where the red hot 'pohakus' (rocks) make the succulent pig 'papaa' (crispy brown).

BAKED MANGOES: Used as a garnish or vegetable.

PAAKAI (HAWAIIAN ROCK SALT): As in ancient times this salt is the residue of evaporated ocean spray and is scraped from rock cavities along the coast line. Sprinkle on your *poi*.

MOA LUAU (CHICKEN WITH TARO LEAVES): Tender Island chicken cooked with taro tops (Hawaiian spinach) and coconut cream, then served in half a coconut shell.

POI (TARO ROOT POUNDED INTO A PASTE): It is the staple food of the Hawaiians, taking the place of bread, and is traditionally eaten with one or two fingers in accompaniment with spicy native dishes.

POI: A grey farinaceous paste made from poi, used as a garnish and condiment.

PUPUS: Hawaiian for hors-d'œuvre.

TARO: Plant used to make a flour for cakes and puddings.

◆ VEGETABLES OAHU: Vegetables cut thinly or diced, sautéd very quickly, remaining crunchy.

PENNSYLVANIA DUTCH

It is often said that the people of the Pennsylvania Dutch country, in the state of Pennsylvania, eat like most American grandmothers did. The plain folk, the Amish, Mennonites and Brethren (Dunkards), groups of religious fundamentalists, have a cuisine which their admirers call simple and substantial and their detractors, coarse and indigestible.

Little has changed since a group of Mennonites from the German Palatinate came to Lancaster county, Pennsylvania, at the invitation of William Penn in 1709. They were followed by several other groups – German, Swiss, French Huguenot and English – who shared literal interpretation of the Bible, anti-militarism and abiding devotion to tilling the land.

The most conservative sects do not have cars, electricity or machinery and till their farms with horse-drawn ploughs. They dress substantially like a peasant of two hundred years ago.

Their food reflects their national origins, their original peasant status and their continued emphasis on thrift and simplicity.

A meal will begin with home-made bread and butter, apple butter and shmierkase, which is creamy cottage cheese, pickled vegetables, bread and butter pickles, green pepper stuffed with chopped cabbage, green gooseberry ketchup and beets. A popular main course is boiled pot pie. Squares of rolled noodle dough are dropped in boiling broth to cook with either chicken, veal, pork or beef. Potatoes and onions are added, and in Lancaster and York counties, saffron. Another popular variation of the pot pie is *Schnitz un Knepp*. Schnitz is sliced dried apple. Two cups of schnitz are simmered with several pounds of ham and molasses 'to taste'. Then the knepp, or button dumplings, leavened with eggs, are dropped in and allowed to steam in a covered pot for 5 or 6 minutes.

These people like to have fruit, pudding and pie for dessert. Pie is a must for every meal. The most famous, Shoofly Pie, is a breakfast pie. Molasses crumb pie, custard pie, funny cake pie, Montgomery-McKinely, 'Quakertown', lemon strip, shell baked custard and vanilla pies are other favourites.

For in-between-meal snacks, pretzels, cookies, cakes and candy, such pastries as fasnachts and plowlines are popular. Plowlines, also called Snavely Sticks, are made from doughnut dough rolled to $\frac{1}{8}$ inch thickness and then fried in deep fat. These used to be taken out to the men in the fields as a mid-morning 'nine-o'clock piece'.

The most talked about feature of this cuisine is the use of various relishes called 'seven sweets and seven sours' although no actual significance is attached to the number. As the cuisine is bland, such foods as spiced canteloup, kümmel cherries, ginger pears, tomato preserves, pepper hash, corn salad, pickled beets, mustard beans, chilli sauce, green tomato pickles, and pickled artichokes add necessary interest.

A SHDREIS'L SUPPE: Literally, hot milk and butter with pretzels broken into it.

AALSUPPE: The familiar Hamburg eel soup.

AARDAPPELEN EN WITEKOOL: A stew of potatoes and white cabbage.

BALKENBRIJ: A kind of scrapple (see Pinhaus, p. 113).

♦ BOOVA SHENKEL: Translated as 'Boy's Leg', it actually is folded circles of pastry dough, filled with a seasoned potato mixture and cooked as dumplings on top of beef stew.

♦ BRAUNE MEHLSUPPE: A meat stock thickened with a brown roux.

♦ BUTTERMILK SOUP: Raisins and cinnamon cooked gently in buttermilk. Served with cream.

COPCHEESE: A sour-milk salted cured cheese that has been aged for a week in a crock. Very similar to German Handkase types.

DAFFODIL CAKE: White cake striped with various coloured batters, usually pink, yellow and chocolate.

DRECHTER KUCHA: A deep fried baked goodie, made from a thin batter dripped from a funnel (Drechter) into hot fat as a criss-crossed strip.

DUTCH GOOSE: A Pennsylvania Dutch dish of stuffed hog maws, which have been braised.

FASTNACHTS: Yeast leavened doughnuts made by the Pennsylvania Dutch on Shrove Tuesday, called Fastnacht day.

FASTNACH KARTOFFEL KUCHEN: A yeast leavened cake made with mashed potatoes and a little flour for binding.

FUNERAL PIE: Raisin pie.

GANNSEKLEIN: A goose stew, actually poached legs, wing tips, etc., with a flour thickened broth.

GOOSE GRIBBEN: Rendered goose skin; *grieben* (German) are the cracklings.

GREEN KERN: They are unripe grain, usually wheat but sometimes rye or barley.

GRUMBIRE SUPPE: Potato soup made with potatoes, onions, and milk and finished with an egg.

G'SHTUPTAFUL LEW'R: Translated as stuffed liver. A split calf's liver, braised with a bread and sage stuffing.

HASENKUCHA: Translated as rabbit cake. Actually, a casserole of picked rabbit meat and seasoned mashed potatoes.

HASSENPFEFFER: A stew made from marinated rabbit.

HOOTSLA: Translated as egg bread. Actually, scrambled eggs, poured on top of fried bread cubes.

KALFGENHAKT: Minced veal.

KARTOFFEL BALLEN: Identical with olivette potatoes.

KARTOFFEL KLOESSE: Potato dumplings.

◆ KARTOFFEL PFANNKUCHEN: Potato pancakes.

KARTOFFEL RÜBEN. Baked potatoes, hollowed out and filled with mashed potatoes.

KNABRUS: Cabbage, shredded finely and cooked in a covered pot with onions.

◆ LIVER DUMPLINGS: Liver blanched and minced. Blended with bread crumbs and seasoning and poached in stock.

LEBANON SAUSAGE: A mixture of chopped leftover meat, potatoes, milk, seasonings, mixed with vinegar.

LOTWERICK: Apple butter.

◆ MANDEL SCHNITZ: A cake made of dried apples and almonds on a sponge cake base.

MORAVIAN CANDY: The confection of one of the Pennsylvania Dutch sects (some of whom also settled in the Carolinas), who seem to specialize in sweets and cakes. They make mints, marzipan, molasses candy brittle, pop corn cake, etc.

OB'L DUNKES KUCHA: An apple sauce cake, leavened by the combination of baking soda and unsweetened apple sauce. (See also Applesauce Cake.)

PEPPERPOT: A soup of distinct German influences containing tripe, vegetables, apples and finished with cream.

PINHAUS: The Pennsylvania Dutch name for Scrapple. (See Philadelphia Scrapple, p. 37.)

PFANNKUCHEN: Pancakes, sprinkled with confectioner's sugar and rolled like crêpes.

RINKTUM DITTY: A sort of fondue.

RIVEL SOUP: A popular soup in Pennsylvania Dutch communities. Made simply with chicken or beef broth with simple flour dumplings (rivels).

ROSINA BOI: A pie made with plain pastry, filled with seeded raisins and topped with a lattice-cross top.

SEVEN SWEETS AND SEVEN SOURS: An assortment of spiced preserves eaten with the plain foods that make up the regimen of the Pennsylvania Dutch people.

SCHNITZ UN KNEPP: Dried apples, ham and dumplings.

SHAKER DRIED CORN: Corn kernels which have been slowly dried in a dutch oven and are hydrated like legumes.

◆ SHOOFLY PIE: A crumb crust filled with a sticky mixture of molasses, brown sugar and seasonings.

◆ SNITZ KLOES: A steamed fruit suet pudding often made from pears, seasoned highly with ginger and cinnamon.

SEMMELS: The Pennsylvania Dutch word for rolls; in this case, yeast leavened rolls, enriched with mashed potatoes, seasoned with sugar and cinnamon.

SOUSE: A sort of head cheese (brawn).

SPECH UND BONA: Ham with green beans and potatoes in water seasoned with vinegar.

◆ SWEET AND SOUR TONGUE: Beef tongue with a sweet-sour sauce.

ZWETSCHENKUCHEN: An open tart filled with plums in a custard mixture.

RECIPES

Some recipes in this book include ingredients which are difficult to obtain in this country, but they have been included as representative of their area and necessary to an overall picture of American cuisine. Other ingredients, including some of the crackers mentioned in the text and tinned shellfish of the kind not readily available fresh, are often obtained from smaller speciality grocery and delicatessen shops.

Clams, used extensively in seaboard recipes, are now more widely available from fishmongers. The American shrimp is not the small variety we know here, the larger prawns are more suitable.

Standard cup measurements are used in the United States. These have been converted into pounds and ounces for dry ingredients, and fluid ounces and pints, as convenient, for liquids. It may be useful to bear in mind that an American cup of liquid is approximately equal to 8 fluid ounces ($1\frac{1}{2}$ gills).

Shortening is any suitable type of fat; use butter, lard, etc., where specified.

Soup

BEAN SOUP
ALL AMERICAN

½ lb. dry beans (kidney beans, split peas, white beans)
3 pts water
ham pieces or ham bone

1 small onion, chopped
2 celery stalks, chopped
1 teaspoon salt
¼ teaspoon pepper

Boil beans in the water for 2 minutes. Remove from the heat. Let soak in cooking water 1 hour or overnight if preferred. Add remaining ingredients. Simmer, covered, until beans are soft, about 2 to 3 hours. Remove ham bone and partially mash beans before serving soup. Serves 6.

BEAN SOUP
WEST

1 lb. dried white beans
5 pts water
meaty ham bone
4 oz. finely chopped onion
½ teaspoon chopped garlic
1 small bay leaf

4 oz. mashed potatoes
4 oz. thin sliced celery
4 oz. diced raw carrots
1 teaspoon salt
½ teaspoon white pepper
4 oz. heavy cream

Wash beans. Bring water to boil in a heavy saucepan. Add beans to water and boil for 2 minutes. Remove from the heat; cover and soak 1 hour. Add ham bone, onion, garlic and bay leaf to beans. Return to heat; bring to boiling point; reduce heat to simmer. Cover tightly; simmer until beans are almost done, about 2 hours. Add potatoes, celery and carrots. Bring to a boil; add salt and pepper. Cover pot and simmer for another hour. Remove the ham bone and cut off the meat. Dice and add to soup. Reheat to boiling. Just before serving, add cream to soup. Serves 6 to 8.

BRAUNE MEHLSUPPE
PENNSYLVANIA DUTCH

2 oz. flour

2 oz. butter

1 teaspoon salt

$\frac{1}{4}$ teaspoon pepper

1$\frac{1}{2}$ pts beef stock

Toast flour in a 350°F oven until brown, about 15 minutes. Combine in a pan over low heat with the melted butter. Slowly stir in the seasonings and stock, stirring constantly. Cook over low heat for 2 hours. Serves 4.

BUTTERMILK SOUP
PENNSYLVANIA DUTCH

1$\frac{1}{2}$ pts buttermilk

1 tablespoon flour

2 oz. seeded raisins

1-inch stick cinnamon

4 tablespoons sugar

$\frac{1}{4}$ pt whipped cream

Combine 1 tablespoon buttermilk with flour. Bring remaining milk to simmer in a pan; stir in buttermilk-flour paste. Wash and drain raisins. Add with seasonings to milk. Cook over very low heat until raisins are plump and soft. Remove the cinnamon stick. Stir in whipped cream. Serve at once. Serves 4.

CREAM OF BROCCOLI SOUP
ALL AMERICAN

1 *package (10 oz.) frozen broccoli*
1 *tablespoon finely chopped onion*
1 *oz. flour*
1¼ *pts vegetable cooking liquid and milk*
½ *oz. butter or margarine*
1½ *teaspoons salt*
pepper
1 *hard-boiled egg, sliced, if desired*

Cook broccoli according to package directions, but omit salt and add onion. Drain; chop; save cooking liquid, make up to 1¼ pts with milk. Mix flour with part of milk mixture until smooth. Add remaining liquid to broccoli. Stir in flour mixture with fat and seasonings. Cook over moderate heat, stirring occasionally, until soup is slightly thickened and flavours are blended. Garnish with slices of hard-boiled egg if desired. Serve with croûtons. Serves 4.

CORN CHOWDER I
NEW ENGLAND

1 *oz. butter*
4 *oz. onion, sliced*
4 *oz. celery, chopped*
1 *lb. cooked potatoes, peeled, diced*
1 *pt milk*
1 *lb. cream-style canned corn*
6 *oz. Cheddar or cantal cheese, grated*
parsley, chopped, for garnish

Melt the butter in a saucepan, and sauté onion and celery until transparent; do not brown. Add potatoes, milk and corn. Heat thoroughly without boiling. Remove from heat and slowly stir in Cheddar cheese. Return to low heat to melt cheese (do not let mixture boil), stir thoroughly. Sprinkle with parsley. Serves 8.

Recipes

CORN CHOWDER II
MIDWEST

3 *slices salt pork*
2 *oz. sliced onion*
6 *oz. sliced potatoes*
$\frac{3}{4}$ *pt water*
8 *large soda crackers*

8 *fl. oz. milk*
1 *lb. cooked corn*
1 *teaspoon salt*
$\frac{1}{4}$ *teaspoon paprika*

Cut salt pork into cubes; brown in a large saucepan. Add onions and cook until browned. Add potatoes and water; cook until potatoes are soft. Mix crackers and milk together; let soak. When potatoes are tender, stir in the crackers, the milk, corn, salt and paprika. Simmer for 15 minutes. Serves 4.

GARBANZO SOUP
SOUTHWEST

1 *lb. chick peas*
2 *ham hocks*
8 *oz. chopped onion*
2 *oz. chopped green pepper*
1 *teaspoon chopped garlic*
1 *tablespoon olive oil*
2 *Spanish sausages (chorizo)*

2 *bay leaves*
$\frac{1}{2}$ *teaspoon Spanish saffron*
$\frac{1}{2}$ *teaspoon black pepper*
$\frac{1}{4}$ *teaspoon salt*
4 *oz. peeled potatoes, cut into eighths*

Wash and soak the beans overnight in water. Rinse the next day. Combine with washed ham hocks and enough cold water to cover mixture. Simmer slowly. Sauté onions, pepper and garlic in olive oil, add to beans, seasonings and sausages. Cook over low heat until beans are tender, about 3 hours. Add potatoes and continue to cook for another hour. (Add water as needed during cooking, but soup should be very thick.) Serves 6 to 8.

HAM BONE SOUP
MOUNTAIN

1 *ham bone*
½ *lb. ham scraps*
¼ *teaspoon black pepper*
⅛ *teaspoon cayenne*
12 *oz. chopped, seeded, peeled tomatoes*

8 *oz. peeled potatoes, cubed*
4 *oz. chopped onion*
4 *pts water*

Boil ham in water with bone and seasonings for 3 hours in a large heavy pot. Add vegetables and cook for another hour. Skim off excess fat from soup. Serve with corn bread. Serves 4 to 6.

MANHATTAN FISH CHOWDER
ALL AMERICAN

1 *lb. fish fillets or steaks, fresh or frozen*
1 *oz. chopped bacon or salt pork*
2 *oz. chopped onion*
¾ *pt boiling water*
1 *can (1 lb.) tomatoes*
4 *oz. diced potatoes*
2 *oz. diced carrots*

2 *oz. chopped celery*
2 *tablespoons ketchup*
1 *tablespoon Worcestershire sauce*
1 *teaspoon salt*
¼ *teaspoon pepper*
¼ *teaspoon thyme*
chopped parsley

Thaw frozen fish. Remove skin and bones. Cut fish into 1-inch pieces. Fry bacon or salt pork in a 5-pint saucepan until crisp. Add onion and cook until tender. Add water, vegetables, ketchup and seasonings except parsley. Cover and simmer 40 to 45 minutes, or until vegetables are tender. Add fish. Cover and simmer about 10 minutes longer, or until fish flakes easily when tested with a fork. Garnish with parsley. Serves 6.

MARYLAND CLAM CHOWDER
MID-ATLANTIC

$2\frac{1}{2}$ pts water
$\frac{1}{2}$ a chicken breast
2 chicken stock cubes
1 stalk celery with top
$\frac{1}{2}$ teaspoon salt
2 oz. carrots, sliced
2 oz. potatoes, diced
2 oz. frozen corn or equivalent
2 oz. frozen peas or equivalent
1 oz. pimento, chopped

2 tablespoons onion, chopped
$\frac{1}{2}$ tablespoon chives, chopped
$\frac{1}{4}$ teaspoon celery salt
$\frac{1}{4}$ teaspoon thyme
$\frac{1}{4}$ teaspoon white pepper
12 shucked whole clams
about 18 soft shell clams
1 gill clam juice
$\frac{1}{2}$ teaspoon parsley, chopped

Combine water, chicken, stock cubes, celery and salt and simmer 1 hour. Discard celery. Remove chicken and finely chop meat, set aside. Add remaining ingredients to stock, except clams, chicken, clam juice and parsley flakes. Simmer 20 minutes. Add remaining ingredients and cook five minutes. Serves 8.

NEW ENGLAND STYLE CLAM CHOWDER
NEW ENGLAND

18 hard shell clams
$1\frac{1}{2}$ gills water
2 oz. lean salt pork, coarse cut
1 oz. butter
2 oz. onion, chopped
2 oz. white of leek, chopped
$1\frac{1}{2}$ pts milk

8 oz. peeled raw potatoes in small fragments
$\frac{1}{2}$ teaspoon Worcestershire sauce
$\frac{1}{2}$ teaspoon salt
$\frac{1}{4}$ teaspoon pepper
8 oyster crackers

Wash clams in several waters. Scrub shells thoroughly. Steam with water in closed pot. Drain clams, reserving liquid.

Remove clams from shells, discarding shell. Finely mince the hard parts of the clams, slice the yellow parts, and coarsely cut pouch. Heat salt pork and butter in heavy-bottomed pan. When fat has melted, cook onions and leeks gently, until soft. Add milk and potatoes, cook 25 minutes until potatoes are done. Add minced clams, ¾ pt of clam liquid (cleared of sand and shell), and seasonings. Cook 10 minutes. Add clam pieces, cook 1 minute. Serve over broken oyster crackers. Serves 6-8.

PEPPER POT SOUP
MID-ATLANTIC

½ *lb. veal (shin)*	2 *bay leaves*
4 *lb. tripe (honeycomb)*	2 *teaspoons salt*
1 *lb. chopped onion*	1 *teaspoon black pepper*
1 *lb. diced potatoes*	½ *teaspoon cayenne pepper*
4 *oz. beef suet*	2 *oz. chopped red pepper*
2 *teaspoons chopped parsley*	10 *oz. flour*
3½ *pints water*	

Cover tripe with water and simmer 1 hour. Drain and cut into ½-inch squares, reserve broth. Simmer veal in broth 3 hours. Remove reserve liquid. Cut meat from bone and dice. Strain broth. Add bay leaves, chopped onions, and simmer 1 hour. Add potatoes, parsley and red pepper. Add meat, pepper, cayenne, and dumplings made of the beef suet, flour and salt mixed together to a paste consistency, and tripe. Cook until dumplings are done. Serves 10.

Recipes

NEW ENGLAND FISH CHOWDER
NEW ENGLAND

1 *lb. fish fillets or steaks, fresh or frozen*	¾ *pt boiling water*
2 *tablespoons chopped bacon or salt pork*	1 *teaspoon salt*
	pepper, as desired
2 *oz. chopped onion*	¾ *pt milk*
¾ *lb. diced potatoes*	½ *oz. butter*
	chopped parsley

Thaw frozen fish; remove skin and bones. Cut fish into 1-inch pieces. Fry bacon or salt pork in a 5-pint saucepan until crisp. Add onion and cook until tender. Add potatoes, water, salt, pepper and fish. Cover; simmer 15 to 20 minutes, or until potatoes are tender. Add milk and butter. Heat; garnish with parsley. Serves 6.

POT LIKKER
MOUNTAIN

1 *bunch turnip tops*	4 *oz. chopped salt pork*
1 *sliced carrot*	1½ *pts water*
1 *sliced turnip*	

Wash turnip tops and place in a pot with other ingredients. Cover with water, boiling slowly until greens are tender. Remove and reserve greens, meat. Drain broth. Season with salt and pepper. Eaten as a soup with corn doggies, corn bread, etc. Meat and greens can be eaten separately.

CREAMY POTATO SOUP
ALL AMERICAN

1½ *lb. raw diced potatoes*	1 *oz. butter or margarine*
1 *oz. finely chopped onion*	2 *teaspoons salt*
¾ *pt water*	*pepper, as desired*
1¼ *pts potato cooking liquid and*	*paprika or chopped parsley*
milk	

Cook potatoes and onion in water in a covered saucepan until potatoes are tender, about 15 minutes. Drain and mash potatoes; save cooking liquid. Measure liquid; add enough milk to make 1¼ pints. Slowly stir liquid into potatoes; add fat and seasonings. Simmer a few minutes to blend flavours. Garnish with paprika or parsley. Serves 6.

TURKEY-VEGETABLE SOUP
ALL AMERICAN

1 *small onion, chopped*	6 *oz. diced potatoes*
1 *oz. butter or margarine*	4 *oz. diced carrots*
¾ *pt water*	1 *pt milk*
2 *chicken bouillon cubes*	1 *oz. flour*
½ *lb. cooked turkey, diced*	1 *teaspoon salt*
2 *oz. celery tops and pieces*	⅛ *teaspoon pepper*

Cook onion in fat until tender. Add water, bouillon cubes, turkey and vegetables. Simmer gently, covered, until vegetables are tender. Stir a little of the milk into the flour until the mixture is smooth; add remaining milk, salt and pepper. Add milk mixture to soup. Simmer, stirring occasionally to prevent sticking, until soup is slightly thickened. Serves 6.

HEARTY VEGETABLE SOUP
ALL AMERICAN

4 oz. cooked beef, cut in small
   pieces
2½ pts beef broth
½ lb. fresh or canned tomatoes
4 oz. diced potatoes
3 oz. diced carrots
2 oz. sliced onions
12 oz. other uncooked vegetables (green peas, chopped
cabbage, diced celery, cut
green beans, chopped green
pepper, sliced okra, diced
turnips, cut corn)
1½ teaspoons salt
⅛ teaspoon pepper

Combine beef and broth in a large saucepan. Add remaining
ingredients. Cook, covered, about 35 minutes or until
vegetables are tender.

VENISON SOUP
MIDWEST

2½ lb. venison (shank, flank,
   neck or breast meat)
6 pts cold water
2 tablespoons salt
1¼ pts tomato juice
6 oz. diced potatoes
4 oz. diced carrots
3 oz. diced celery
2 oz. finely chopped onion
2 tablespoons finely chopped
   parsley
1 tablespoon sugar
½ teaspoon savory
¼ teaspoon pepper

Simmer meat in water with salt for 2 hours or until very
tender. Skim occasionally. Let broth stand overnight. Remove
congealed fat; add vegetables and other ingredients. Simmer
2 hours over low heat. Serves 8.

VIRGINIA PEANUT SOUP
MID-ATLANTIC

1 *oz. butter*
1 *oz. onion, chopped*
1 *oz. celery, chopped*
1 *oz. flour*
8 *fl. oz. chicken stock*
¼ *bay leaf*

1 *sprig parsley*
1½ *pts milk*
8 *oz. peanut butter*
¼ *teaspoon pepper*
1 *oz. grated nuts*

Melt 1 ounce butter in heavy-bottomed pan. Sauté onion and celery until transparent but not browned. Add flour and cook until golden. Moisten slowly with chicken stock. Add bay leaf and parsley. Cook 15 minutes. Strain, add milk, bring to a boil. Remove from heat. Stir in peanut butter, return to heat but do not boil. Cook gently for 15 minutes. Add pepper if necessary (some peanut butter is very salty). Sprinkle grated nuts on top just before serving. Serves 6.

Shellfish

CRAB MEAT STUFFED PEPPERS
CREOLE

1 *lb. crab meat*
6 *green peppers*
1 *pt boiling water*
1 *teaspoon salt*
2 *tablespoons mayonnaise*
2 *eggs, hard-boiled and chopped*

1 *tablespoon chilli sauce*
2 *tablespoons lemon juice*
dash Worcestershire sauce
dash tabasco sauce
1 *tablespoon chilli sauce*

Remove any shell or cartilage from crab meat. Cut stem ends from peppers; remove seeds and membrane. Wash peppers; add salt to boiling water; cook peppers in water for 4 minutes. Drain. Combine crab meat, mayonnaise, eggs, half chilli sauce, lemon juice and seasonings. Fill peppers. Place in a well-greased round baking dish. Bake in a pre-heated 425°F oven until brown, about 25 minutes. Garnish each pepper with 2 teaspoons of the remaining chilli sauce. Serves 6.

STUFFED KING CRAB LEGS
FARWEST

2 *packages (12 oz. each) pre-cooked frozen King Crab legs*
1 *oz. butter*
2 *oz. cooked mushrooms*
2 *tablespoons flour*

½ *teaspoon salt*
8 *fl. oz. milk*
2 *oz. mild grated cheese*
paprika

Shellfish

Thaw frozen legs. With a sharp knife, slit open legs and remove meat from shells. Reserve the shells. Pick over meat for shell and cartilage. Cut the meat into ½-inch pieces. In a heavy pan, melt the butter; add mushrooms; sprinkle with flour to make a light vegetable roux. Add the milk to the roux; cook over low heat, stirring constantly for 15 minutes. Add the cheese gradually and the crab meat. Heat through. Fill the shells with the mixture and place in a baking pan. Sprinkle with paprika; bake in a pre-heated 350 °F oven for 10 minutes. Serves 6.

CRABURGERS
FARWEST

½ lb. flaked crab meat
4 oz. grated sharp Cheddar cheese
3 tablespoons mayonnaise
3 tablespoons chilli sauce
2 hard-boiled eggs, chopped
3 tablespoons chopped ripe pimento olives
1 tablespoon lemon juice
½ teaspoon monosodium glutamate
½ teaspoon garlic salt
½ teaspoon paprika
¼ teaspoon celery salt
¼ teaspoon ground thyme
4 soft buns or 8 slices of toasted bread

Combine crab meat with all other ingredients except the buns in a mixing bowl. Mix together well. Spread the crab mixture on split buns or on the toast. Bake at 400 °F for 10 minutes. Grill until lightly browned, about 5 minutes. Serves 8.

Recipes

DEVILLED CRAB
MID-ATLANTIC

1 *lb. crab meat*
6 *oz. cracker crumbs*
2½ *oz. melted butter*
2 *oz. onion, chopped*
1 *tablespoon parsley, chopped*
2 *fl. oz. evaporated milk*
1 *tablespoon lemon juice*
1 *teaspoon Worcestershire sauce*

1 *teaspoon dry mustard*
½ *teaspoon salt*
¼ *teaspoon white pepper*
3 *drops red pepper sauce*
6 *ramekins or cleaned, emptied crab shells*
1½ *oz. butter*

Combine all ingredients well except 2 oz. cracker crumbs. Fill ramekins. Sprinkle with remaining cracker crumbs and dot with butter. Bake in a 375 °F oven until brown, about 15 minutes. Serves 6.

CRAB IMPERIAL
MID-ATLANTIC

1 *oz. flour*
1 *oz. butter*
6 *fl. oz. milk*
1 *lb. backfin crab meat, canned or fresh*
1 *beaten egg*
1 *hard-boiled egg, chopped fine*
1 *tablespoon mayonnaise*
6 *drops Worcestershire sauce*

½ *teaspoon dry mustard*
⅙ *teaspoon cayenne*
¼ *teaspoon white pepper*
½ *teaspoon chopped parsley*
2 *oz. bread crumbs, dried*
2 *oz. butter*
6 *strips pimento (tinned)*
6 *ramekins or cleaned crab shells*

Make a white roux with flour and 2 tablespoons of butter. Add the milk; stir until thick. Simmer gently 5 minutes. Reserve 6 tablespoons of the mixture. Combine the crab meat, raw egg, boiled egg, mayonnaise, Worcestershire sauce, mustard, seasonings, parsley and remaining white sauce. Mix lightly but thoroughly. Pack crab mixture into ramekins or shells.

130

Sprinkle with bread crumbs, 2 oz. butter and reserved sauce. Decorate with pimento strips. Bake in a 350 °F oven till brown, about 20 minutes. Serves 6.

CRAB AND OKRA GUMBO
CREOLE

4 *cooked crabs to make* 1 *lb.*
  crab meat
2 *oz. raw ham*
3 *slices bacon*
2 *tablespoons flour*
2 *tablespoons salad oil*
1 *lb. cooked, cleaned, de-veined*
  shrimps

4 *green onions, chopped*
1 *teaspoon chopped garlic*
¾ *pt boiling water*
1 *lb. washed okra, stemmed and*
  cut fine
2 *tablespoons tomato paste*
3 *oz. hot cooked rice*

Clean the crabs, and remove meat from claws and body. Cut ham and bacon into small pieces. Make a light roux of flour and oil in a large pan. Add ham and bacon to the roux and cook the mixture for 2 minutes. Add the shrimps and crab to the mixture and cook for 15 minutes. Now add the garlic and onion. Slowly add the water and bring the mixture to a boil. Add the okra and tomato paste. Reduce the heat and cover the pan. Simmer for 1 hour or until relatively thick. Place rice in six bowls. Spoon gumbo mixture over it. Serves 6.

CLAM SOUFFLÉ
FARWEST

12 *soda crackers*
8 *fl. oz. milk*
2 *eggs, well beaten*
7 *oz. minced canned clams with*
  liquid or 7 *oz. cooked fresh*
  clams, minced with liquor

2 *tablespoons melted butter*
1 *teaspoon grated onion*
1 *teaspoon chopped parsley*
1 *teaspoon salt*
¼ *teaspoon white pepper*

Soak the soda crackers in milk in a dish for 20 minutes. Add eggs, clams, butter, onion, parsley, salt and white pepper. Stir mixture well and pour it into a buttered baking dish. Bake the mixture at 350 °F until it is set and browned, about 35 minutes. Serves 6.

SPICED CRAYFISH
CREOLE

8 *dozen crayfish*
3 *bay leaves*
1 *clove garlic, chopped*
2 *teaspoons allspice*
1 *teaspoon nutmeg*
½ *teaspoon cayenne pepper*

3 *pts cold water*
4 *oz. salt*
1 *tablespoon chopped onion*
2 *tablespoons lemon juice*
3 *tablespoons Worcestershire sauce*

Kill crayfish by immersing quickly in boiling water. Clean by twisting off middle tail flipper and pulling to remove intestinal trace. Put spices in a muslin bag or cheese cloth bag. Bring 3 pts of water to a boil with salt, onion, lemon juice and Worcestershire sauce. Add crayfish and spice bag. Bring water to a boil again; boil for 5 minutes. Drain and rinse the crayfish for 2 minutes in cold water. Chill crayfish and serve. Serves 4.

CRAYFISH STEW
CREOLE

2½ *lb. crayfish meat*
2 *oz. cooking oil*
2 *oz. flour*
6 *oz. chopped onion*
2 *oz. green pepper, finely chopped*

½ *teaspoon chopped garlic*
6 *drops tabasco sauce*
1 *tablespoon chopped spring onions*
1 *tablespoon chopped parsley*

Make a dark roux of oil and flour. Add onions, green pepper and garlic and cook until translucent. Add crayfish meat and hot sauce, cooking until the mixture is a thick stew, about 45 minutes. Add spring onions and parsley and serve with French bread. Makes 8 to 10 servings.

LOBSTER NEWBURG
MID-ATLANTIC

1½ *lb. cooked picked lobster*	2 *egg yolks, beaten*
1½ *oz. butter*	¼ *teaspoon salt*
8 *fl. oz. sherry*	*pinch of cayenne pepper*
½ *teaspoon paprika*	6 *slices of toast in quarters,*
8 *fl. oz. heavy cream*	*optional*

Cook lobster in butter in a saucepan over very low heat until it colours bright red. Add wine and paprika (the paprika is mainly for colour), and simmer until wine has been reduced to a tablespoonful. Add cream to mixture; cook over low heat for 3 minutes. Slowly add egg yolks to lobster with seasonings. Cook over low heat for a moment until mixture thickens. Lobster Newburg can be poured over toast points to serve, or it can be served in half lobster shells. Serves 6.

BUTTERED LOBSTER
NEW ENGLAND

1 *lb. diced lobster meat, cooked or canned*	1 *teaspoon parsley, chopped*
2 *oz. butter, melted*	½ *teaspoon powdered mustard or* 1 *teaspoon French mustard*
1 *teaspoon Worcestershire sauce*	½ *teaspoon paprika*
1 *teaspoon lemon juice*	½ *teaspoon salt*

If canned lobster is used drain thoroughly. Combine all ingredients in a heavy-bottomed saucepan. Heat gently until hot. Serve in hot or warm vol-au-vent cases.

OYSTERS ROCKEFELLER
CREOLE

36 *oysters, shucked*	2½ *oz. butter*
36 *deep oyster shells, scrubbed*	½ *teaspoon salt*
½ *lb. washed spinach or other*	½ *bay leaf*
greens	6 *drops red pepper sauce*
1 *tablespoon parsley*	1 *tablespoon anise liqueur*
1 *green onion top*	1 *oz. bread crumbs*
3 *tablespoons onion, chopped*	*rock salt*

Partially fill a medium-large baking pan that can go to table with gravel or salt. This will provide a bed for the oyster shells. Pass spinach, parsley, onion top and onions through a food mill or whirl in a blender for 10 seconds at high speed. Put this mixture in a frying pan with butter and cook for 5 minutes. Mix the cooked mixture with seasonings. Place the oyster shells in the baking pan. Place a small dab of spinach mixture in each shell. Place an oyster on top of the spinach. Place under the grill for 3 minutes or until oyster edges begin to curl. Meanwhile, combine the remaining spinach mixture with the bread crumbs. Fill cooked oysters in the shells with the mixture. Return the baking pan to a pre-heated 400 °F oven until mixture is slightly brown, about 10 minutes. Serves 6.

OYSTER STEW
MID-ATLANTIC

1½ pts of shelled oysters in cooking liquid
1½ pts light cream
2 oz. butter
¼ teaspoon Worcestershire sauce
4 drops tabasco sauce
paprika
oyster crackers

Heat oysters in liquid until edges begin to curl. Heat cream very hot. Combine all ingredients except paprika and oyster crackers, cook 30 seconds. Pour into bowls and sprinkle with paprika. Serve at once with oyster crackers. Serves 8.

OYSTER FRITTERS
MID-ATLANTIC

3 dozen medium-sized oysters
4 oz. flour
1 teaspoon salt
¼ teaspoon cayenne pepper
1 gill water
2 tablespoons salad oil
1 egg yolk, beaten
1 egg white, beaten stiff
tartar sauce
deep fat for frying

Drain oysters thoroughly. Spread out on paper towels to dry. Sift dry ingredients together. Combine water, oil and egg yolk. Gradually add to dry ingredients with a minimum of stirring. Allow batter to stand 1 hour. Fold in egg white. Dip oysters in batter, fry in 375 °F fat until golden brown, about 3 minutes. Drain on kitchen paper. Serve with tartar sauce. Serves 6.

Tartar Sauce

8 fl. oz. home-made or com-
    mercial mayonnaise
3 tablespoons sweet pickle
    relish
1 tablespoon capers, chopped

1 tablespoon onion, chopped
$\frac{1}{2}$ teaspoon lemon juice
$\frac{1}{2}$ teaspoon prepared mustard
3 drops Worcestershire sauce
2 drops tabasco sauce

Combine all ingredients.

OYSTER LOAF SANDWICH
CREOLE

2 dozen fresh oysters, shelled
2 eggs, well-beaten
$\frac{1}{2}$ gill milk
$\frac{1}{2}$ cup cracker crumbs
1 loaf day-old French bread

$2\frac{1}{2}$ oz. butter
1 dill pickle, sliced
3 tablespoons melted butter
oil for deep frying

Pat oysters dry with paper towelling. Combine milk and eggs
in a bowl. Dip the oysters first in milk and egg mixture, then
in cracker crumbs. Slice top off bread lengthwise. Hollow the
resulting 'boat' and the inside of the top. Smear bread
generously with butter and toast it in a 400 °F oven. While the
bread is toasting, deep fry the oysters. Fill toasted bread with
oysters, top with the melted butter and sliced pickle. Slice loaf
into 4 sections. Garnish with olives, raw celery, radishes, etc.,
if desired. Serves 4.

SCALLOPED OYSTERS
NEW ENGLAND

2 oz. fresh bread crumbs	1 teaspoon salt
4 oz. melted butter	⅛ teaspoon grated nutmeg
2 tablespoons chopped parsley	3 tablespoons grated Parmesan
1½ pts oysters	cheese
8 fl. oz. double cream	1 tablespoon paprika
2 tablespoons drained, chopped pimento	

Combine the bread crumbs, butter and parsley in a thick-bottomed pan. Toss to mix; heat until hazelnut smell develops. Layer some of the bread crumb mixture on the bottom of a buttered baking dish. Alternate bread crumbs, drained oysters, cream, salt, pepper, nutmeg and pimento until the dish is full. Sprinkle the top layer with combination of cheese and paprika. Bake in a pre-heated 400°F oven until top is browned and oysters are cooked, about 30 minutes. Serves 6.

HANGTOWN FRY
FARWEST

12 small oysters	1 oz. grated onion
2 oz. cracker crumbs	½ teaspoon grated garlic
1½ oz. butter	6 drops red pepper sauce
2 oz. chopped ham	8 eggs

Dip the oysters in cracker crumbs and reserve. Break the eggs in a bowl and beat in chopped onion, ham and seasonings. Heat butter in a large frying pan. Quickly brown the oysters in the butter and add egg mixture to pan. Slowly fry over low heat until eggs are set. Turn mixture once. Serve at once. Serves 4.

Recipes

BAY SCALLOPS
(These are very small scallops)
MID-ATLANTIC

3 *cups bay scallops (tiny*
scallops, use only abductor
muscle and white parts)
2 *tablespoons flour*
½ *teaspoon salt*
⅓ *teaspoon white pepper*

¼ *teaspoon paprika*
1 *oz. bacon fat*
1 *oz. butter*
1 *teaspoon lemon juice*
1 *tablespoon parsley, chopped*

Drain scallops. Combine flour, salt, pepper and paprika. Dust
scallops lightly with flour mixture. In a heavy pan, heat fat
until hot but not smoking. Fry the scallops 2 minutes on
each side. Remove them from the pan to a heated platter. Pour
fat off from pan and melt butter, browning it slightly. Add the
lemon juice and parsley to the melted butter and then pour
mixture over the scallops. Serve at once. Serves 4.

CLASSIC SHRIMP GUMBO
CREOLE

4 *oz. bacon drippings*
2 *oz. plain flour*
4 *oz. chopped onion*
2½ *pts warm water*
3 *lb. raw clean shrimps (these*
are Jumbo shrimp, about
size of large prawns)

½ *lb. fresh okra, sliced*
1 *teaspoon filé [see page 52]*
1 *teaspoon salt*
½ *teaspoon white pepper*

Make a very dark roux with the bacon drippings and flour in a
heavy-bottomed pot. Add chopped onions and cook until they
are transparent. Add the water and slowly bring the mixture
to a boil. Add the shrimps and okra. Boil 15 minutes. Reduce

138

heat; simmer 14 minutes. Remove pan from heat; add filé, salt and pepper. Allow to cool and develop overnight. The next day, bring to a simmer but do not boil. Serves 6.

SHRIMP CREOLE
CREOLE

1 *lb. raw, peeled, de-veined shrimps (Jumbo shrimp)*
1 *oz. bacon fat*
1 *oz. flour*
1½ *gills hot water*
1 *can (8 oz.) tomato sauce*
2 *oz. chopped spring onions and tops*
2 *tablespoons chopped parsley*

1 *tablespoon chopped green pepper*
4 *cloves of garlic, finely chopped*
1½ *teaspoons salt*
½ *teaspoon crushed whole thyme*
2 *whole bay leaves*
1 *lemon slice*
dash cayenne pepper

Cut shrimps in half if large. In a heavy-bottomed pan, make a light roux of the flour and bacon fat. Gradually add the water to the roux and cook over a low heat until thick, stirring the mixture constantly. Add the remaining ingredients to the mixture. Cover the pan and simmer the Creole for 20 minutes. Remove the bay leaves. Serve on hot rice. Serves 6.

BUTTERFLY SHRIMP ALOHA NUI LOAH
HAWAIIAN

2 *lb. of large shrimps*
1 *tablespoon cornflower*
2 *oz. flour*
1 *teaspoon baking powder*
½ *teaspoon monosodium gluta-mate*

2 *tablespoons water*
1 *egg, well beaten*
1 *teaspoon salt*

Combine all the ingredients, except the shrimps, into a batter. Split the cleaned raw shrimps, with shells and veins removed, down their backs to within half an inch of their tails. Dip shrimps in the batter and drop into deep hot fat. Cook until brown. Drain on paper towels and serve at once with Apricot Sauce Honi (see p. 219). Serves a party of 10 to 12.

JAMBALAYA
This can be made with other varieties of fish and shellfish, as available
CREOLE

1 *tablespoon lard*
8 *oz. ham in ½-inch cubes*
4 *oz. mild pork sausage in slices*
4 *oz. hot pork sausage in slices*
1 *green pepper, skinned, seeded and chopped*
1 *sweet red pepper, skinned, seeded and chopped*
1 *clove garlic, crushed*
1 *tablespoon flour*
8 *oz. cooked cleaned shrimps*
8 *oz. crab meat*
8 *oz. cleaned crayfish tails*
1 *lb. tomatoes, skinned, seeded and chopped*
1 *large onion, chopped fine*
1 *tablespoon celery tops, blanched and chopped*

1 *pt water or stock from cooking shellfish*
1 *teaspoon Pernod*
1 *lb. long-grain raw rice*
2 *tablespoons parsley, blanched and chopped*
1 *tablespoon Worcestershire sauce*
1 *teaspoon salt*
½ *teaspoon dried thyme*
¼ *teaspoon gumbo file (powdered bay leaves and sassafras)*
6 *drops red hot sauce*
pinch chilli powder
pinch red pepper (optional)
8 *cooked crayfish tails*

Melt lard in a large pan. Add ham, sausage and green and red peppers. Cook until pepper has softened and the sausage is browned. Add the garlic; cook 1 minute. Add flour by sprinkling over the fat; stir well. Cook 2 minutes. Add shrimp, crab meat, uncooked crayfish, tomatoes, onions, celery, water and Pernod. Bring to a boil. Boil for five minutes. Add all other ingredients except the eight crayfish in the shell. Cover and cook in a moderate oven until rice has absorbed all the liquid, about 35 minutes. Serve with a crayfish on top of each portion. Makes 8 servings.

Fish

SMOKED CARP
MIDWEST

6 *lb. whole carp*
½ *lb. salt*
4¾ *pts water*

3½ *oz. brown sugar*
home smoker (directions below)

Remove carp skin and scales with a sharp knife. Remove dorsal fin by cutting the roots out. Clean, wash and drain the fish. Split lengthwise; cut each half in 6 pieces. Mix the salt water and brown sugar, pour over carp and let stand overnight. Remove fish and place in a home smoker for three hours.

Home Smoker
Run metal rods or wire clothes hangers three-quarters of the way up a five-gallon covered container (usually a lard tin is used). Punch two ½-inch holes in the top to let the smoke out slowly. Punch hole in the base to allow good ventilation of fire from below. Support can on bricks. Build a small charcoal fire in base. When coals are white, add pieces of apple wood, hickory or other aromatic branches (as long as they have no resins).

CATFISH (OR FISH) GUMBO
CREOLE

1 *lb. skinned catfish fillets or other fillets, fresh or frozen*	1 *can (1 lb.) whole tomatoes*
4 *oz. chopped celery*	1 *package (10 oz.) frozen okra or 10 oz. fresh okra*
2 *oz. chopped green pepper*	2 *teaspoons salt*
2 *oz. chopped onion*	$\frac{1}{4}$ *teaspoon white pepper*
1 *clove garlic, finely chopped*	$\frac{1}{4}$ *teaspoon thyme*
2 *oz. bacon fat*	$\frac{1}{2}$ *bay leaf*
2 *beef bouillon cubes*	1 *dash tabasco sauce*
$\frac{3}{4}$ *pt boiling water*	4 *oz. hot cooked rice*

Cut fish fillets into 1-inch pieces. Sauté celery, green pepper, onion and garlic in fat until transparent but not brown in a pan. Dissolve bouillon cubes in water. Add bouillon, tomatoes, okra and seasonings to pan. Cover and simmer 30 minutes. Add fish; cover and simmer until fish is done, about 15 minutes. Remove bay leaf. Place tablespoon rice in each soup bowl. Fill with gumbo. Serves 6.

FRIED CATFISH
MOUNTAIN

6 *skinned catfish (or other bottom-feeding river fish)*	2 *eggs, slightly beaten*
2 *teaspoons salt*	2 *tablespoons milk*
$\frac{1}{4}$ *teaspoon pepper*	*cornmeal*
	2 *tablespoons bacon fat*

Sprinkle both sides of fish with salt and pepper. Combine eggs and milk in bowl. Dip fish in egg mixture and roll in cornmeal. Melt fat in pan until hot but not smoking (should cover pan about $\frac{1}{8}$ inch deep). Place fish in pan and fry at moderate heat. Turn to brown other side. Cook about 10 minutes in all.

CAPE COD TURKEY (COD FISH BALLS)
NEW ENGLAND

1 *lb. salt cod with skin and bones*
½ *lb. raw potatoes, finely chopped*

1 *whole egg*
1 *egg yolk*
1 *tablespoon butter*
pinch cayenne pepper

Soak cod overnight, rinse in several waters. Simmer 15 minutes, discard skin and bones. Drain. Boil potatoes. Drain. Mash, or pass through food mill with the fish. Add well-beaten egg and egg yolk, butter and cayenne. Beat until mixture is light and smooth. Form small balls on a spoon, like quenelles, and drop the balls into very hot fat (385 °F), a few at a time, without allowing balls to touch. Remove as soon as balls are brown. Drain on kitchen paper. Makes about 35 balls.

CREAMED COD
NEW ENGLAND

1 *lb. salt cod*
1 *oz. flour*
1 *oz. butter*
¾ *pt milk*
¼ *teaspoon white pepper*
pinch grated nutmeg

1 *egg yolk, beaten*
6 *slices of white toast without crusts*
boiled potatoes
parsley, chopped, to garnish

Soak cod overnight. Rinse in several waters. Drain and break into small pieces. Melt butter, add flour. Add milk little by little and simmer 20 minutes. Add cod and seasoning to sauce, cook 10 minutes. Add egg yolk away from the fire, do not boil. Serve on toast with boiled potatoes, sprinkled with chopped parsley. Serves 6.

BAKED FISH FILLETS OR STEAKS
ALL AMERICAN

2 lb. white fish fillets or steaks, fresh or frozen
2 tablespoons melted fat or oil
2 tablespoons lemon juice
1 teaspoon salt
½ teaspoon paprika
pepper as desired

Thaw frozen fish. Cut into 6 portions. Place fish in a single layer, skin side down, in a well-greased baking dish. Combine remaining ingredients and pour over fish. Bake at 350°F, 20 to 25 minutes, or until fish flakes easily when tested with a fork. Serves 6.

COURT BOUILLON
CREOLE

5 lb. Gaspergou (sheepshead) red fish or fresh cod
6 tablespoons oil
6 tablespoons flour
8 oz. chopped onion
2 cans (1 lb.) whole tomatoes, crushed
3 tablespoons chopped green pepper
2 tablespoons chopped garlic
2 pts water
1 tablespoon chopped celery tops
1 can (8 oz.) tomato sauce
1 tablespoon chopped parsley
2 tablespoons chopped spring onion

Cut the fish into large chunks. Make a brown roux of the oil and flour in a heavy-bottomed pan. Add onions, cooked until soft. Add tomatoes, garlic, green pepper; cook 15 minutes.

Add water, celery tops; bring mixture to a boil. Add tomato sauce; lower flame to simmer; cook 1 hour. Add fish. Cook until fish is done. Serve over rice, garnished with chopped parsley and spring onion. Serves 8.

BARBECUED HALIBUT STEAKS
FARWEST

2 *lb. halibut steaks*
1 *oz. chopped onion*
2 *tablespoons chopped green pepper*
½ *teaspoon chopped garlic*
1 *oz. melted bacon fat*
8 *fl. oz. tomato sauce*

2 *tablespoons lemon juice*
1 *tablespoon Worcestershire sauce*
1 *tablespoon sugar*
2 *teaspoons salt*
¼ *teaspoon pepper*

Cut the steaks into convenient serving-size pieces. In a large pan, cook the onion, green pepper and garlic in the bacon fat until tender. Add remaining ingredients except the fish and simmer it over low heat for about 5 minutes. Cool the resulting sauce. Marinate the fish in sauce mixture for 30 minutes. Remove fish and grill about 7 minutes on each side. Serves 6.

OVEN FRIED PERCH
MIDWEST

2 *lb. perch fillets [if small, use whole fish]*
4 *oz. butter, melted*
⅛ *teaspoon celery salt*

⅛ *teaspoon onion salt*
1/16 *teaspoon garlic salt*
2 *oz. cornflakes, crushed*
2 *oz. potato crisps, crushed*

Wash and dry fillets; dip in butter that has been mixed with seasoned salts. Roll the fillets in a mixture of cornflakes and potato crisps. Place in an oven dish that can go to the table. Bake in a 375 °F oven until well browned, about 20 minutes. Serves 4 to 6.

STUFFED ROCKFISH
MID-ATLANTIC

4 *oz. celery, dried*
2 *oz. onion, chopped*
4 *oz. butter*
6 *slices white bread without crusts, crumbled*
1 *teaspoon parsley, chopped*
¼ *teaspoon poultry seasoning or powdered thyme*

½ *teaspoon salt*
¼ *teaspoon white pepper*
1 *3-lb. rockfish (sea bass or bream)*
2 *strips bacon*

Sauté celery and onion in butter until transparent but not brown. Add bread crumbs, parsley flakes and poultry seasoning. Combine thoroughly. Season with salt and pepper. Stuff rockfish and sew belly. Cover with bacon strips. Place in a dish that can go to the table and bake in a 350 °F oven for 1 hour. Discard thread. Serves 6.

SALMON LOAF
ALL AMERICAN

1 *can (1 lb.) salmon*
4 *fl. oz. milk*
4 *oz. soft bread crumbs*
2 *oz. butter or margarine, melted*
½ *gill salmon liquid*
3 *egg yolks, beaten*

2 *tablespoons finely chopped green pepper*
2 *tablespoons finely chopped onion*
1 *tablespoon lemon juice*
⅛ *teaspoon pepper*
3 *egg whites, stiffly beaten*

Drain salmon; save the liquid. Flake salmon. Heat milk, add bread crumbs and butter or margarine and let stand 5 minutes.

Add salmon liquid and beat until smooth. Add egg yolks, green pepper, onion, lemon juice, pepper and salmon; mix well. Fold in egg whites. Pour into a well-greased loaf tin. Bake in a 350 °F oven 40 to 50 minutes or until firm in centre. Remove from oven; let stand 5 minutes. Loosen from sides of pan with spatula; invert on a serving platter. Serve plain or with a sauce. Serves 6.

LOMI LOMI SALMON
HAWAIIAN

1½ lb. fresh salmon in one piece
½ lb. salt
1 lb. chopped peeled tomatoes
2 oz. chopped spring onions
1 tablespoon lemon juice

Sprinkle salt on salmon and allow to pickle overnight. The next day, wash off salt; bone and shred salmon. Before serving, combine salmon with remaining ingredients in a serving dish.

BAKED SHAD
NEW ENGLAND

2 oz. fresh white bread crumbs
2 fl. oz. milk
½ onion, chopped
4 oz. celery, chopped
2 tablespoons bacon fat
1 medium-sized shad roe
1 egg
1 tablespoon parsley, chopped
½ teaspoon salt
¼ teaspoon white pepper
4 lb. shad, boned but head and tail on
½ lb. streaky bacon

Combine bread crumbs and milk. Sauté onion and celery in bacon fat. Blanch shad roe very quickly in boiling water. Chop coarsely. Combine all ingredients except salt pork, stuff fish and sew up. Place on buttered baking dish that can go to table. Place sliced bacon over fish. Bake in a 350 °F oven for 45 minutes. Remove threads. Serves 8.

Note: If shad is unavailable, any fresh fish of the herring family can be used. Canned roe may be substituted with fairly good results.

SHAD ROE
MID-ATLANTIC

1½ *pts water*	½ *teaspoon salt*
1 *tablespoon vinegar*	¼ *teaspoon pepper*
1 *teaspoon salt*	*deep fat for frying*
6 *shad roe (or other available*	1½ *oz. melted butter*
fresh roe or milt)	6 *rashers fried bacon*
1 *oz. flour*	

Bring water, vinegar and 1 teaspoon salt to a boil. Reduce heat to simmer, add shad roe. Cook 15 minutes. Drain. Rinse shad roe under cold water for 5 minutes. Drain. Combine flour, remaining salt and pepper. Dip roe in flour. Fry in 375 °F fat until brown, about 3 minutes. Pour on melted butter. Serve with bacon slices. Serves 6.

SMELT SMOKIES
MIDWEST

1½ *to* 2 *lb. cleaned smelt*	3 *tablespoons dry milk powder*
juice of 2 *lemons*	2 *teaspoons grated horseradish*
2 *oz. flour*	2 *tablespoons smoked salt*
1½ *oz. cornmeal*	*deep fat for frying*

Clean and wash fish thoroughly. Soak fish in lemon juice for 15 minutes. Drain fish. Combine remaining ingredients in a plastic or paper bag. Put fish in bag; shake well to coat thoroughly. Shake off excess. Deep fry in 370 °F fat until well browned, about 3 minutes. Serves 4.

BROILED RAINBOW TROUT
WEST

6 *trout*
2 *tablespoons lemon juice*
2 *oz. butter*
½ *teaspoon salt*

⅛ *teaspoon coarsely ground pepper*
1 *tablespoon chopped parsley*

Clean fish and pat dry. Combine butter, lemon juice and seasonings. Rub fish with butter mixture. Grill under medium heat a few minutes on each side. Baste with the drippings. Serve with chopped parsley on top.

TUNA PIE
ALL AMERICAN

1 *can (6½ or 7 oz.) tuna*
2 *tablespoons chopped onion*
1 *tablespoon tuna oil*
1 *can (10½ oz.) condensed cream of mushroom soup*

2 *eggs beaten*
½ *oz. soft bread crumbs*
6 *thin slices lemon or orange*
1 *package (12 oz.) corn bread or corn muffin mix*

Drain tuna; save oil. Flake tuna. Cook onion in oil until tender. Add soup, eggs, bread crumbs and tuna; mix well. Arrange lemon or orange slices on the bottom of a well-greased 10-inch flan tin. Pour tuna mixture over fruit slices. Prepare cornbread mix as directed on package. Spread batter over tuna mixture. Bake at 400 °F for 25 to 30 minutes or until brown. Remove from oven; let stand 5 minutes. Loosen from sides with a spatula and invert on a serving plate. Serves 6.

CHILLI COLORADO CON TORTITAS DE HUEVO
(to serve with fried fish)
SOUTHWEST

1 *tablespoon flour*
8 *fl. oz. chilli sauce*
8 *fl. oz. water*
1 *clove garlic*

3 *eggs, separated*
8 *oz. lard plus* 1 *extra table-spoon*

Heat 1 tablespoon of lard in a pan; add flour, mix in chilli sauce and water; simmer over low heat with the finely chopped garlic for about 3 minutes. Beat egg whites stiff in a bowl. Add the egg yolks and continue to beat for 2 minutes. Heat remaining lard in a heavy frying pan. Drop in egg mixture by teaspoonfuls; turn once. Drop fried egg pieces into prepared chilli sauce.

Beef

BARBECUED BEEF SHORTRIBS
WEST

3 lb. beef shortribs
2 tablespoons lard
2 oz. chopped onion
8 fl. oz. tomato ketchup
4 fl. oz. water
3 tablespoons brown sugar

2 tablespoons Worcestershire
sauce
2 teaspoons salt
1 teaspoon mustard
$\frac{1}{4}$ teaspoon vinegar

Have butcher cut ribs into 3-inch sections. Brown in lard with
chopped onion in a heavy pan. Combine remaining ingredients.
Add to ribs. Cover and bake in a moderate 350 °F oven until
tender, about 2 hours. Serves 4.

BARBECUED BEEF SANDWICHES
ALL AMERICAN

1$\frac{1}{2}$ lb. ground beef
4 oz. chopped onion
4 oz. chopped celery
1 can (8 oz.) Spanish-style
tomato sauce
2 fl. oz. ketchup
2 tablespoons brown sugar,
packed

2 tablespoons vinegar
2 tablespoons barbecue sauce
1 tablespoon Worcestershire
sauce
1 tablespoon prepared mustard
2 tablespoons salt
pepper, as desired
6 hamburger buns

152

Crumble beef into saucepan and brown lightly. Drain off excess fat. Mix in onion and celery. Combine tomato sauce, ketchup, brown sugar, vinegar, barbecue sauce and seasonings in a bowl. Pour over meat; cover pan; simmer barbecue 1½ to 2 hours or until flavours are well blended. Spoon beef mixture over buns. Serves 6.

BEEF STEW
ALL AMERICAN

1½ oz. flour	3 medium-sized onions, sliced
1½ teaspoons salt	4 medium-sized potatoes, cut in 1-inch cubes
⅛ teaspoon pepper	
1½ lb. stewing beef, cut in 1-inch cubes	5 medium-sized carrots, quartered
2 tablespoons fat or oil	8 oz. frozen peas
1¼ pts water	½ gill water

Combine flour, salt and pepper in a bowl. Coat meat with seasoned flour. Save remaining flour. Brown meat in hot fat in a large saucepan. Add water and cover tightly. Simmer until meat is tender, about 1½ hours. Add onions, potatoes, and carrots. Cover and simmer 15 minutes. Add peas. Cover and simmer until all vegetables are tender. Blend ½ gill water with remaining flour. Add to stew, stirring gently. Cook until thickened. Serves 6.

BOOVA SHENKEL
PENNSYLVANIA DUTCH

3 lb. beef for stew	2 teaspoons baking powder
12 medium potatoes	½ teaspoon salt
6 tablespoons butter	4 tablespoons cold water
2 tablespoons chopped parsley	1 cup dry bread, in pieces
1 oz. chopped onion	1 gill milk
3 eggs	4 oz. shortening
10 oz. sifted flour	

Cover meat with water. Add seasonings, simmer 3 hours. Peel potatoes, cut into thin slices, cover with water, cook until tender. Drain, add half butter, salt and pepper to taste, parsley, chopped onion. Beat eggs, add to potatoes and beat mixture lightly together. Sift together flour, baking powder and salt. Cut in shortening using two knives, add enough water to make very stiff dough. Roll very thin on floured board and cut into 10-inch circles. Spread with some of the potato mixture. Fold dough into semi-circle, crimp edges with prongs of a fork. Place on top of meat and broth, cover, boil about 30 minutes. Melt remaining butter, stir bread pieces into it, then milk. Arrange meat, with dough semi-circles on top, pour milk sauce over. Serves 10.

BUL KOGI
HAWAIIAN

2 to 3 lb. sirloin steak or top sirloin roast
2 fl. oz. soy sauce
1 oz. sugar
1 tablespoon vegetable oil

½ clove garlic, mixed
2 stalks scallions, chopped
½ teaspoon monosodium glutamate

Meat should be cut across the grain into fillets about ⅛ inch thick. Combine the other ingredients into a marinade and mix well. Marinate each piece of meat for 30 minutes and grill quickly. Bul Kogi is best when cooked just before serving, but for preparation in advance, steak fillets may be marinated, grilled, covered and refrigerated. If this is done, remove the cover and heat in medium oven (350°F) for five minutes before serving.

CHILLI
SOUTHWEST

2 fl. oz. olive oil
4 oz. chopped onion
4 oz. chopped green peppers
4 oz. chopped, peeled and seeded tomatoes
8 fl. oz. tomato sauce
1 teaspoon chopped garlic
2 lb. lean beef, cut into pieces the size of a sugar cube

2 tablespoons chilli powder
1 tablespoon paprika
1 teaspoon salt
½ teaspoon white pepper
½ teaspoon powdered oregano
¼ teaspoon cumin seed
1½ oz. corn meal
2 fl. oz. water

Heat olive oil in a heavy-bottomed pan. Add beef and brown well. Sauté vegetables. Add all other ingredients except corn meal and water. Simmer over low heat, stirring occasionally for 2 hours. Combine cornmeal with cold water. Slowly combine with beef mixture, stirring well. Cook 3 minutes over low heat. Makes 1½ quarts. Used as all-purpose sauce, or with rice, beans, macaroni, crackers as a main dish. Also used for tostados, chiles rellenos.

MEAT LOAF
ALL AMERICAN

1½ lb. ground beef
3 slices soft white bread, torn into very small pieces
8 fl. oz. tomato juice or milk

2 oz. finely chopped onion
1 egg, beaten
1 teaspoon salt
¼ teaspoon pepper

Mix ingredients thoroughly. Press into a 9 by 5 by 3 inch baking tin or shape into a loaf. Bake uncovered at 350°F (moderate oven) about 1½ hours. Remove from oven and drain off excess fat. Serves 6.

NEW ENGLAND BOILED DINNER
NEW ENGLAND

8 *small onions*	½ *lb. salt pork*
8 *small potatoes*	½ *lb. ham or pork tenderloin*
8 *small beetroots*	1 *large onion stuck with a clove*
2 *large turnips in eighths*	1 *small cabbage, quartered*
3 *lb. corned beef (in England this would be salted brisket)*	

Peel vegetables. Soak meat in cold running water for 30 minutes. Cook meat in water at a simmer, with onion and clove, until done, about 3 hours. Meanwhile cook vegetables separately in boiling water (except cabbage). Fifteen minutes before meat is done, combine all ingredients including cabbage. Finish cooking. Drain and slice meats, garnish with vegetables. Serves 8.

Leftovers are used for Red Flannel Hash (see p. 158).

BRAISED OXTAIL
WEST

1 *oxtail, about 3 lb.*	½ *teaspoon powdered cloves*
1 *oz. flour*	¼ *teaspoon white pepper*
1 *oz. butter*	12 *oz. diced carrots*
8 *fl. oz. beef broth or water*	2 *oz. chopped onion*
½ *lb. chopped, peeled, seeded tomatoes*	1 *oz. turnip*
1 *teaspoon salt*	*juice of* 1 *lemon*

Cut oxtail at joints. Roll in flour. Melt ½ oz. butter in a pan. Brown the oxtail; add water, tomatoes and seasoning; simmer until tender, about 2 hours. Brown vegetables in a pan with the remaining butter. Add to meat; cook 30 minutes. De-grease. Finish with lemon juice to taste. Serves 4–5.

QUICK BEEF PIE
ALL AMERICAN

1½ lb. ground beef
1 medium-sized onion, chopped
½ teaspoon salt
1 can (10½ oz.) condensed
   tomato soup

1 can (1 lb.) cut green beans,
   drained
¼ teaspoon pepper
1 lb. seasoned mashed potatoes
½ cup shredded Cheddar cheese

Crumble beef into large frying pan. Add onion and salt; cook until browned. Drain off excess fat. Add soup, green beans and pepper; simmer 5 minutes. Pour into greased 2-quart casserole. Drop potatoes in mounds onto hot meat mixture. Sprinkle with cheese. Bake at 350 °F (moderate oven) for 20 minutes. Serves 6.

BEEF STROGANOFF
ALL AMERICAN

1½ oz. flour
1 teaspoon salt
¼ teaspoon pepper
1 lb. sirloin tip steak, cut in
   very thin strips
2 oz. finely chopped onion
2 oz. fat or oil
1 can (10½ oz.) condensed
   cream of mushroom soup

1 can (8 oz.) sliced mushrooms,
   drained
8 oz. sour cream
cooked rice
paprika
parsley

Combine flour, salt and pepper. Coat meat strips with flour mixture. Brown meat in hot fat in a large frying pan. Add onion and cook until clear. Drain off excess fat. Add soup and mushrooms. Simmer, covered, 10 to 15 minutes. Blend in sour cream and remove from heat. Serve over rice. Sprinkle with paprika and garnish with parsley. Serves 6.

RED FLANNEL HASH
NEW ENGLAND

1 *lb. cooked potatoes, diced*	3 *tablespoons bacon drippings*
¾ *lb. cooked beets, chopped*	2 *fl. oz. water*
4 *oz. cooked turnip, chopped*	1 *tablespoon heavy cream*
8 *oz. cooked corned beef* (p. 156)	¼ *teaspoon white pepper*

Brown vegetables and meat in fat. Add water, cover, and simmer 20 minutes. Add cream and pepper, increase heat and brown one side of mixture, pressing occasionally with spatula to give it omelette-like form. Brown other side and serve. Serves 6.

TAMALE LOAF
SOUTHWEST

5 *oz. cornmeal*	1 *oz. bacon fat*
2½ *pts water*	8 *oz. canned tomatoes*
1 *teaspoon salt*	4 *oz. pitted chopped green olives*
1 *lb. ground beef*	
2 *oz. chopped green pepper*	1 *tablespoon chilli powder*
2 *oz. chopped onions*	½ *teaspoon white pepper*
½ *teaspoon chopped garlic*	

Combine cornmeal, water and salt in a mixing bowl. Brown meat, peppers, onion, garlic in bacon fat. Combine mixture with other ingredients. Bake in a greased loaf pan in a 400 °F oven until top has browned, about 30 minutes.

SWEET AND SOUR TONGUE
PENNSYLVANIA DUTCH

1 *smoked beef tongue*	2 *oz. gingersnap crumbs*
1 *bay leaf about 1 inch long*	3½ *oz. brown sugar*
½ *tablespoon black peppercorns*	1 *tablespoon vinegar*
1½ *pts water*	2 *oz. seeded raisins*

Soak the tongue in water overnight. Discard the soaking water. Cover the tongue in a pan with 1½ pints water, bay leaf, peppercorns; simmer until tender, about 4 hours. Skin tongue, remove gristle and fat, slice. Combine 1 cup strained stock from cooking broth, with gingersnaps, brown sugar and vinegar. Cook over low heat until smooth. Add the raisins and pour over the sliced tongue.

BEEF BRAINS WITH EGGS
WEST

1 *beef or 2 veal brains*	¼ *teaspoon white pepper*
2 *tablespoons butter*	5 *eggs*
1 *tablespoon grated onion*	2 *tablespoons chopped parsley*
2 *teaspoons salt*	4 *slices toasted bread*

Soak the brains in cold running water for half an hour. Clean thoroughly. Chop into small pieces. Heat butter in a frying pan; add onion and seasonings. Brown brains in the butter; cook over low heat for 10 minutes. Beat eggs in a bowl with parsley. Pour over the brains in the frying pan, stir until eggs are set. Serve on toast. Serves 4.

LIVER DUMPLINGS
PENNSYLVANIA DUTCH

$1\frac{1}{2}$ *lb. calves' liver*
$\frac{3}{4}$ *pt water*
2 *tablespoons bacon fat*
4 *oz. chopped onion*
$\frac{1}{4}$ *teaspoon sage*
$\frac{1}{2}$ *teaspoon salt*

$\frac{1}{2}$ *teaspoon white pepper*
2 *eggs*
4 *oz. bread crumbs*
1 *oz. flour*
$\frac{3}{4}$ *pt soup stock*

Cut up liver. Simmer in water in a pan for 5 minutes. Drain; mince. Fry onion in bacon fat in a pan. Combine liver, seasonings and eggs in a bowl. Toast the bread crumbs with the onions in fat. Add the bread crumb mixture to the liver mixture, binding with flour as necessary. Shape into dumplings. Poach in soup stock in a covered pot for about 30 minutes. Serve with sauerkraut. Serves 6.

STUFFED GREEN PEPPERS
ALL AMERICAN

3 *large green peppers*
2 *teaspoons salt*
boiling water
1 *lb. ground beef*
4 *oz. rice, cooked*
2 *tablespoons finely chopped celery*
2 *tablespoons finely chopped onion*

2 *tablespoons chilli sauce*
2 *teaspoons salt*
$\frac{1}{4}$ *teaspoon pepper*
1 *egg*
2 *tablespoons grated Cheddar cheese*

Halve peppers lengthwise; remove stems, seeds and membranes. Add 2 teaspoons salt to enough boiling water to cover peppers; boil 5 minutes. Drain. Combine other ingredients except cheese; mix well. Fill pepper halves with this mixture and place in $\frac{1}{2}$ inch hot water in a baking pan. Bake uncovered at 350°F (moderate oven) 45 to 55 minutes. Sprinkle cheese over peppers and bake 5 minutes longer, or just until cheese melts. Serves 6.

Pork

BACKBONE WITH NOODLES
MOUNTAIN

1 *pork backbone*
¾ *pt boiling water*
4 *oz. chopped onion*
2 *tablespoons flour*

1 *teaspoon salt*
½ *teaspoon black pepper*
¾ *lb. noodles*

Wash backbone and cut into pieces. Cover with boiling water in baking dish. Add onions and cook for 2 hours in a moderate oven (350°F). Remove meat from pan and de-grease cooking liquid. Add flour and seasonings to pan and thicken liquid to a gravy consistency. Return pork to pan and heat. Serve over hot cooked noodles.

CARNE ABOBADA
SOUTHWEST

1 *pt chilli sauce* (p. 220)
1 *tablespoon oregano*
2 *teaspoons salt*

1 *clove chopped garlic*
3 *lb. pork chops*
4 *oz. fat*

Combine all ingredients except pork and fat, mix well. Then add pork to mixture and allow to stand 24 hours. Remove meat from sauce. Fry in fat, then add sauce; cook until done, about 1 hour.

CHILES RELLENOS
SOUTHWEST

6 *large green peppers*   5 *beaten eggs*
deep fat for frying
filling for tostados (see page
  170)

Plunge peppers in 350°F fat until they are cooked, about 8 minutes. Remove skins, seeds, stems. Fill with cooked meat mixture, packing it well. Dip in beaten eggs, and fry in 375°F fat until browned, about 3 minutes. Serves 6.

CHITTERLINGS I
MOUNTAIN

8 *lb. chitterlings (the small*   1 *red chilli pepper*
  intestine of pigs)   2 *cloves garlic*
4 *pts water*   *flour*
1 *tablespoon salt*   *deep fat for frying*
1 *tablespoon black pepper*

Clean chitterlings thoroughly, leaving some of the fat. Put them in a large pot with the other ingredients, except the fat and flour. Cook until tender enough to pull apart. Cut into 1-inch pieces. Flour and deep fry.

CHITTERLINGS II
MOUNTAIN

3 *lb. chitterlings (the small*   ½ *bay leaf*
  intestine of pigs)   2 *eggs*
1 *tablespoon salt*   1 *tablespoon water*
1½ *pts water*   1 *cup cracker crumbs*
½ *teaspoon crushed red pepper*   *deep fat for frying*

Wash chitterlings (they should be bought cleaned). Cook in boiling salted water with bay leaf and red pepper until tender, about 2 hours. Drain; cut into 1-inch squares. Beat egg with 1 tablespoon water. Dip chitterlings into egg mixture and then into cracker crumbs. Fry in 350 °F fat until brown, about 3 minutes. Serves 6.

CORNMEAL MUSH WITH PORK
MOUNTAIN

1 *lb. lean pork with bones (spareribs)*	5 *oz. cornmeal*
3 *pts water*	1 *teaspoon salt*
	½ *teaspoon powdered sage*

Put pork in a heavy saucepan, add water and simmer until meat falls from bones. Remove meat and chill. Cool broth and remove fat. Measure skimmed broth and add or remove liquid until there is one quart. In a saucepan, combine broth and cornmeal and cook, stirring frequently until thick. Chop meat, add seasonings and add to mush. Stir to mix. Pack in bread pans and chill. To serve, slice and sauté. Serves 6.

HOG JOWL, GREENS, POT LIKKER, AND CORN PONE
MOUNTAIN

2 *lb. hog jowl*	5 *oz. white cornmeal*
1½ *pts water*	2 *tablespoons bacon fat*
1 *gallon greens (turnip, collard, etc.)*	½ *teaspoon salt*
	2 *oz. cold water*

Wash hog jowl in several waters. Boil for 45 minutes in a heavy saucepan in 1½ pts of water. Wash greens and add to boiling hog jowl; cook for an additional hour. Remove greens, drain and chop very coarsely. Combine cornmeal, salt and bacon fat with enough cold water to make a stiff dough. Form into twelve small dumplings; poach in pot likker, at a simmer, for 20 minutes. Slice hog jowl; arrange on a hot platter with greens and corn pone. Moisten with 2 cups of pot likker. Serves 6 to 8.

N.B.—A ¾-pound piece of salt pork can be substituted for hog jowl. The corn pone is also often baked in a greased tin in a hot oven for 20 minutes.

HOPPING JOHN
SOUTH

¾ *lb. yellow peas*
¼ *lb. pork (salt pork, pig tails, etc.)*
1¼ *pts water*
8 *oz. long-grain rice*

1½ *oz. butter*
1 *teaspoon salt (more or less, depending on saltiness of pork)*
½ *teaspoon pepper*

Soak peas overnight in water. Drain thoroughly and wash. Drain well again. Place peas, pork and water in a pot; cook until peas are done, about 2 hours. Drain. Measure cooking liquid and adjust to ¾ pint. Add rice, butter, salt and pepper. Bring mixture to a boil, stir. Mix peas, pork and rice in a buttered baking dish. Bake in a 350 °F oven until rice is done, about 40 minutes. Serves 8.

LAULAU
HAWAIIAN

3 *lb. fresh pork, shoulder or leg*
1½ *lb. salted butterfish (or other salt fish)*
36 *luau (taro) or fresh spinach leaves*

2 *tablespoons rock salt*
12 *ti leaves (or use large, outer cabbage leaves)*
6 *cooking bananas*
6 *sweet potatoes*

Divide pork and fish into six equal portions, one portion per laulau. Wash luau leaves thoroughly, through several waters. Strip stem and fibrous part of veins from back of leaves by pulling gently with the tip of a knife from stem to edge of leaves; discard stem and veins. If butterfish is very salty, soak for several hours. Place pork in bowl, add salt, work together thoroughly. Arrange 5 or more luau leaves, the largest on the bottom, in the palm of hand. If using spinach, arrange a small handful of spinach in a flat layer. Add pork, with fat side up; then a layer of butterfish. Fold luau leaves or ends of spinach over pork and fish to form a bundle (puolo). Prepare each ti leaf by cutting the stiff rib partially through and stripping it off. Place bundles on the end of a ti leaf and wrap tightly. Wrap another leaf around in the opposite direction, forming a flat package. Tie securely with string or the fibrous part of the ti leaves. Repeat procedure for the other five laulaus. Steam laulaus for 4 to 5 hours; add sweet potatoes and bananas for the last hour. Remove string from laulaus and serve.

NECKBONES AND CORN MUSH
MOUNTAIN

2 *lb. neck bones of pork*
1½ *pts water*
5 *oz. white cornmeal*

½ *teaspoon powdered sage*
1 *teaspoon salt*
1 *teaspoon black pepper*

Simmer neck bones in a pan with water until meat falls away from the bone. Remove bones and meat; discard bones; chop meat. Cool liquid and remove fat. Adjust to 1½ pints liquid volume with added water. Bring to a simmer; pour in cornmeal. Cook mixture over low heat until thick. Add seasonings and chopped meat; pack in loaf pans and chill. Cut into slices when ready to use and fry.

PHILADELPHIA SCRAPPLE
MID-ATLANTIC

2 *lb. lean bony pork (shanks,*	½ *teaspoon sage*
etc.)	¼ *teaspoon grated nutmeg*
1 *tablespoon salt*	5 *oz. white cornmeal*
½ *teaspoon coarse black pepper*	2 *oz. buckwheat flour*
2½ *pts cold water*	¾ *pt cold water*

Simmer pork with salt and pepper in the cold water in a heavy pan until it is tender (about 2 hours). Skim top occasionally. Strain the broth and reserve. Remove the bones from the meat. Chop the meat fine and return to the broth. Add sage and nutmeg to meat. Combine cornmeal and buckwheat flour in a bowl with two cups of cold water; mix until lumps disappear. Bring broth to a boil; slowly add the cornmeal mixture, keeping the broth at a boil. Simmer for 1 hour, stirring occasionally. Then pour mixture into loaf pans until it reaches 3 inches in depth. Chill mixture until firm. To serve, turn scrapple out of pan; slice and fry in a heavy frying pan.

PICKLED PIG'S FEET
MOUNTAIN

4 *pig's feet*
1¼ *pts vinegar*
1½ *pts water*
4 *oz. chopped onion*
12 *black peppercorns*

3 *whole cloves*
1 *bay leaf*
1 *tablespoon salt*
½ *red chilli pepper*

Wash pig's feet under running water; slit. Cover with vinegar and cold water. Add seasonings and simmer 2½ hours, skimming constantly. Cool in liquid. Serve cold.

PIG TAILS AND BEANS
MOUNTAIN

3 *lb. pig tails*
1 *lb. navy beans*

3 *oz. chopped onion*
½ *chilli pepper*

Cook meat in water to cover until tender, about 2 hours; remove meat from bones. Soak beans overnight. Cook beans with onions, seasonings in broth from meat until tender, about 2 hours. Add meat to beans and cook over low heat until water is almost gone.

SALT PORK WITH MILK GRAVY
MOUNTAIN

1 *lb. salt pork*
1½ *pts water*
3 *tablespoons flour*

¾ *pt milk*
¼ *teaspoon white pepper*

Pork

Wash the salt pork in several waters. Place in a pan and cover with water. Soak overnight. Drain and place in a saucepan with 1½ pints of water; simmer for 30 minutes. Drain pork again. Dice and then slowly fry very crisp in a heavy pot. Remove and keep warm. Pour off all but 3 tablespoons of fat. Make a light roux with the fat and flour. Add the milk to the pan; simmer 10 minutes, add the pepper and pour over pork.

SOUR RIBS
MOUNTAIN

3 *lb. spareribs*
1 *gill water*
½ *gill vinegar*
4 *oz. finely chopped onion*

1½ *gills tomato ketchup*
½ *teaspoon tabasco sauce*
2 *tablespoons black strap molasses*

Pre-heat oven to 375 °F. Cut ribs into single ribs and place in baking pan. Cook for 1 hour with 1 gill water. Drain off liquid and fat. Combine remaining ingredients. Pour mixture over ribs and cook for 1½ hours more, basting frequently.

SUCCOTASH
NEW ENGLAND

2 *oz. salt pork, diced*
1 *tablespoon flour*
¼ *pt cream*
½ *lb. cooked small lima beans, or flageolet*

1 *large boiled turnip, diced*
½ *lb. corn, cooked*
¼ *teaspoon white pepper*

Render salt pork, but do not brown. Sprinkle with flour to make light roux. Add cream, cook 5 minutes. Add vegetables and seasonings. Simmer 5 minutes. Serves 6.

TOSTADOS
SOUTHWEST

2 *lb. lean pork, ground*
2 *fl. oz. white vinegar*
1 *tablespoon salt*
1 *teaspoon grated garlic*

1 *tablespoon chilli powder*
8 *taco shells (see p. 264)*
2 *oz. shredded lettuce*
3 *oz. grated cheese*

Place pork in a bowl; add vinegar to moisten well. Mix with hands and let set for 1 hour. Add salt; mix well. Add grated garlic and mix thoroughly. Add chilli powder and continue to mix. Let season in refrigerator overnight. Cook in a medium-hot pan over low heat for 1 hour. Serve in taco shells topped with shredded lettuce and grated cheese.

Ham

GRILLED HAM LEILANI
HAWAIIAN

cloves
ham steak, thickness according
   to taste
3–4 slices fresh or canned
   pineapple

Bul Kogi barbecue sauce (see
   p. 215)

Insert cloves into ham steak and place in open baking dish. Cover with slices of pineapple. Cook in medium oven (440–450°F) for about 20 minutes, basting several times with Bul Kogi barbecue sauce as it cooks. When ham is cooked, place under grill for a few minutes until it is browned.

HAM PATTIES
ALL AMERICAN

$\frac{1}{2}$ lb. ground cooked ham
4 oz. mashed potatoes
1 tablespoon chopped onion
$\frac{1}{4}$ teaspoon dry mustard
$\frac{1}{4}$ teaspoon salt

1 tablespoon milk
1 egg beaten
fine dry bread crumbs
3 tablespoons fat or oil

Combine ground ham, mashed potatoes, onion, mustard, and $\frac{1}{4}$ teaspoon salt. Chill about 1 hour. Shape into 12 patties.

Blend milk into beaten egg. Dip patties in egg mixture and
then in crumbs. Fry patties in hot fat until golden brown.
Serve with egg sauce. Serves 6.

HOMINY AND BACON
MOUNTAIN

$\frac{1}{2}$ *lb. cooked hominy grits*	*2 tablespoons bacon fat*
2 oz. chopped onion	*1 tablespoon sugar*
1 oz. chopped green pepper	*1 teaspoon salt*
$\frac{1}{2}$ *lb. chopped and seeded, peeled*	*5 drops red pepper sauce*
tomatoes	*8 slices bacon*

Place hominy in a well-greased baking dish. Sauté vegetables
in a pan with bacon fat. Combine with seasonings and spoon
over hominy. Place bacon slices on top; bake in a moderate
325 °F oven until bacon is crisp, about 30 minutes.

SMITHFIELD VIRGINIA HAM
MID-ATLANTIC

1 Virginia (Smithfield) ham or	*4 fl. oz. sherry*
other country ham	*2 dozen whole cloves*
2 lb. 4$\frac{1}{2}$ oz. brown sugar	
4 fl. oz. prepared mustard	

Soak ham for 24 hours in water. Change water at least three
times during soaking. Wash and scrub ham under running
water using a wire brush. Put ham in a large pan and cover
with water and 2 pounds of brown sugar. Cook at a high
simmer, replenishing water as needed, for about 18 minutes
per pound, until small bone at base of ham can be pulled
loose. Cool ham in its own liquid; remove skin and trim fat.
Combine mustard, 4$\frac{1}{2}$ oz. brown sugar and sherry in a bowl to
make a thick jam-like paste. Spread over fatty portion of the

ham. Stud the ham with cloves in an even, decorative pattern. Bake ham in medium oven until crust is well browned, about 1 to 1½ hours. Baste during cooking with pan drippings. Serve cold in very thin slices.

COUNTRY HAM WITH RED-EYE GRAVY
MOUNTAIN

2 *centre cut ham slices,* ⅜ *inch thick*
cold water

1 *tablespoon flour*
½ *gill freshly brewed coffee*

Soak ham slices for 30 minutes in cold water. Dry thoroughly. Place slices of ham in a heavy frying pan; if the ham is very lean, add a little fat. Cook slowly until done, about 15 minutes. Add flour to pan juices, moisten with coffee and cook for 3 minutes, stirring constantly. Serve gravy over grits or biscuits with the ham. Serves 4.

PLANTATION DINNER
SOUTH

1 *slice of ham, about an inch thick*
3 *cloves*
¼ *teaspoon grated nutmeg*
6 *oz. honey*

2 *fl. oz. water*
4 *oz. sliced cooked parsnips*
4 *oz. sliced cooked sweet potatoes*

Spike the ham with cloves; sprinkle with nutmeg. Place in a greased baking pan. Cover with honey and water. Cover pan and bake in a pre-heated 325 °F oven until tender, about 45 minutes. Remove from oven; cover ham with alternate layers of parsnips and sweet potatoes. Bake uncovered until top layer of vegetables is browned, about 10 minutes. Serves 4.

Lamb and Veal

DEVILLED LAMB RIBS
WEST

3 *lb. lamb ribs, in 2-inch pieces*
2 *tablespoons mustard*
4 *oz. flour*
1 *teaspoon salt*
¼ *teaspoon white pepper*
2½ *oz. butter*
¾ *pt water*

4 *fl. oz. chilli sauce*
juice of 1 lemon
2 *tablespoons Worcestershire sauce*
½ *teaspoon paprika*
¼ *teaspoon grated onion*
3 *¼-inch lemon slices*

Brush ribs with mustard. Sprinkle with flour, salt and pepper. Melt butter in pan. Brown lamb. Combine remaining ingredients and pour over lamb. Cook over low heat until lamb is done, about 1 hour. Serves 4.

GRILLADE PANNÉ
CREOLE

4 *slices fillet or oyster of veal, about ½ inch thick*
¼ *teaspoon white pepper*
2 *eggs, well beaten*
pinch powdered red pepper

2 *tablespoons grated onion*
1 *oz. cornmeal*
fat for deep frying
tomato gravy (recipe below)

174

Trim meat and cut it into 3-inch strips. Sprinkle with pepper. Combine eggs, red pepper and grated onion. Marinate meat in egg mixture for about 2 hours. Dip each piece of veal in the cornmeal. Heat fat in heavy-bottomed pan to 350°F. Deep fry veal strips until brown and tender, about 4 minutes. Serve with tomato gravy. Serves 4.

Tomato Gravy

2 tablespoons flour	1 tablespoon sweet pepper
2 tablespoons oil	$\frac{1}{2}$ teaspoon salt
1 tablespoon chopped garlic	$\frac{1}{2}$ teaspoon sugar
$\frac{1}{2}$ chopped onion	$\frac{1}{4}$ teaspoon red pepper powder
1 can (4 oz.) whole tomatoes	$1\frac{1}{2}$ gills water

In a heavy pan, make a dark brown roux of the flour and oil. Add the garlic and onion and cook until transparent. Crush the tomatoes. Add the tomatoes and juice to the onion mixture. Cook 30 minutes. Add seasonings and water and bring to a boil. Simmer over low heat for 15 minutes.

Game

FRIED RABBIT
MID-ATLANTIC

1 *rabbit*	2 *fl. oz. milk*
1 *oz. flour*	4 *oz. dry bread crumbs*
$\frac{1}{2}$ *teaspoon paprika*	2 *oz. butter*
$\frac{1}{2}$ *teaspoon salt*	2 *fl. oz. water*
1 *egg*	

Clean rabbit and cut into small pieces. Combine flour, paprika and salt and sprinkle over rabbit. Beat egg and milk together. Dip rabbit in mixture then in bread crumbs. Melt the butter, brown rabbit pieces. Add water, cover closely and place in 355 °F oven. Cook until tender. Thicken drippings if necessary with a little flour. Sour cream can be added just before serving. Serves 4.

BARBECUED RABBIT
SOUTHWEST

1 *2-lb. rabbit*	$\frac{1}{4}$ *teaspoon white pepper*
1 *oz. flour*	3 *tablespoons bacon fat*
$\frac{1}{2}$ *teaspoon salt*	*barbecue sauce (recipe below)*

Joint the rabbit. Mix the flour, salt and pepper together. Roll the rabbit pieces in this mixture. Heat the fat in a pan.

176

Brown the rabbit on all sides over moderate heat, about 20 minutes. Pour Barbecue Sauce over the rabbit. Cover the pan. Bake in 325 °F oven until meat is tender, about 45 minutes. Uncover pan and place under grill until meat is brown, about 15 minutes. Serves 4.

Barbecue Sauce

8 *fl. oz. tomato juice*
2 *oz. chopped onion*
2 *tablespoons ketchup*
2 *tablespoons vinegar*
2 *tablespoons brown sugar*
1 *tablespoon paprika*

1 *teaspoon salt*
1 *teaspoon dry mustard*
¼ *teaspoon chilli powder*
2 *tablespoons Worcestershire sauce*

Combine all ingredients in a saucepan. Cook over low heat for 15 minutes.

RABBIT STEW
MIDWEST

1 *rabbit*
1¼ *pts water*
1 *teaspoon salt*
2 *oz. butter*
4 *oz. potatoes, cut in julienne strips*
2 *oz. celery in julienne strips*

2 *oz. carrots in julienne strips*
2 *oz. chopped onion*
8 *fl. oz. tomato sauce*
3 *tablespoons chopped parsley*
1 *oz. flour*
½ *gill cold water*

Cover rabbit with water and add salt in a large pan. Stew until tender, about 1½ hours. Drain and remove meat; reduce broth to 2 cups and reserve. When meat has cooled, bone and cut coarsely. Melt butter in frying pan; add potatoes, celery, carrot and onion. Cover and cook gently 15 minutes. Add broth and tomato sauce; bring to a boil. Add meat and parsley to mixture. Combine flour and cold water in a cup.

Add slowly to stew, stirring well. Cook an additional 15 minutes. Serves 4 to 6.

VENISON CHILLI
SOUTHWEST

$\frac{3}{4}$ *lb. bacon*
1$\frac{1}{2}$ *lb. ground venison*
1$\frac{1}{2}$ *pts cooked red kidney beans*
2 *lb. canned tomatoes*
$\frac{1}{2}$ *lb. chopped onion*

$\frac{1}{2}$ *tablespoon salt*
$\frac{1}{2}$ *tablespoon chilli powder*
$\frac{3}{4}$ *teaspoon pepper*
$\frac{1}{4}$ *teaspoon cumin*

Cut bacon in small pieces; brown crisp in heavy-bottomed pan. Add venison and brown. Combine rest of ingredients. Add to browned meat with enough water to cover mixture. Simmer for 2 hours. Serves 10.

VENISON SAUSAGE
SOUTHWEST

3 *oz. salt*
$\frac{3}{5}$ *oz. black pepper*
$\frac{2}{5}$ *oz. sage*
$\frac{1}{5}$ *oz. red pepper*

6 *lb. venison*
2 *lb. lean pork*
2 *lb. fat pork*

Sprinkle seasonings over meat. Mince twice. Make into patties. Freeze and use as needed. Will keep up to three months. Makes 10 pounds.

CORNED VENISON
WEST

6 *pts hot water*
1$\frac{1}{2}$ *lb. salt*
$\frac{1}{2}$ *lb. brown sugar*
1 *oz. baking soda*

1 *oz. cream of tartar*
1 *oz. pickling spices*
2 *boned shoulders of venison, in 3-lb. pieces*

Make a brine of all the ingredients except the meat; cool. Place meat in a stone crock and pour brine over it to cover meat. Weight meat down with a clean board and a weight. Tie a cheese cloth over the top. Keep in a cool place. Meat will be cured in three weeks.

VENISON SWISS STEAK
WEST

1½ *lb. round of venison, cut into steaks* 1½ *inch thick*	6 *oz. chopped onion*
2 *oz. flour*	6 *oz. tomatoes*
1 *teaspoon salt*	1 *oz. chopped celery*
½ *teaspoon white pepper*	2 *tablespoons Worcestershire sauce*
1 *oz. bacon fat*	

Dredge steaks with flour and season with salt and pepper. Melt bacon fat in a heavy pan and brown steak in fat on both sides. Add other ingredients to pan. Cover tightly and cook in a 350°F oven until tender, about 1½ hours. Remove meat to platter; clear some of the grease from pan liquid. Use liquid as a gravy. Serve with baked potatoes. Serves 4.

GROUSE IN WINE SAUCE
MIDWEST

2 *grouse*	8 *oz. flour*
1 *bottle port or red wine*	1½ *teaspoons salt*
2 *whole cloves*	1 *teaspoon black pepper*
4 *oz. chopped onion*	1 *teaspoon sage*
1 *large bay leaf*	

After birds have been thoroughly cleaned and singed, cut into pieces. Combine wine, cloves, onion and bay leaf in a large bowl. Place the grouse pieces in this wine mixture to marinate for three days in the refrigerator. Drain birds, reserving marinade. Wipe dry and dip in flour combined with salt and pepper. Brown on both sides in butter. Combine birds and reserved marinade in a casserole. Bake in a pre-heated 300 °F oven for about 1 hour or until tender. Serves 4.

SMOTHERED PHEASANT
WEST

1 *large pheasant*	1 *oz. chopped onion*
4 *oz. flour*	1 *can (6 oz.) condensed mush-*
1½ *teaspoons salt*	*room soup*
1 *teaspoon black pepper*	2 *tablespoons flour*
4 *oz. butter*	*milk*
1 *pt cream*	

Thoroughly clean and singe bird. Joint. Mix flour with salt and pepper in a dish. Dredge bird. Melt butter in a heavy frying pan. Brown pheasant. Add cream and onion; simmer until tender, about 1 hour. Remove meat from gravy; strain. Add mushroom soup and flour moistened with a little milk. Return the pheasant to the sauce; simmer until a thick sauce develops, about 15 minutes. Serves 4 to 6.

PIEDMONT DOVE
(or any small game bird)
SOUTH

4 *doves, trussed but not cut up*	2 *oz. chopped celery*
(use squab, or young pigeon)	1 *teaspoon salt*
1 *oz. flour*	½ *teaspoon pepper*
4 *rashers bacon*	¼ *teaspoon thyme*
4 *oz. chopped onion*	8 *fl. oz. sherry*

Game

Flour birds lightly. Render bacon in a frying pan; remove meat. Add butter to the bacon fat; sauté onion and celery until transparent. Brown birds with vegetables. Remove from heat; add thyme and half of the sherry. Place in a casserole, bake in a 350°F oven, baste with cooking juice adding remaining sherry. Cook until tender about 40 minutes. Garnish with bacon strips. Serves 4 to 6.

WILD DUCK
SOUTH

2 wild ducks (only ducks smelling of fish should be soaked and parboiled)	1 teaspoon pepper
	4 apples
	4 oranges
2 tablespoons salt	8 stalks celery
6½ pts water	8 fl. oz. sherry
1 chopped onion	bacon fat and butter (see
1 teaspoon salt	recipe)

Soak ducks for 1 hour in 2 quarts of water with 2 tablespoons of salt, rinse. In large pan, bring 2 quarts of water to a boil, add the onion, the ducks and cook for 3 minutes. Remove, and drain the ducks, dry thoroughly with cloth or paper towels. Combine salt and pepper; rub ducks inside and out. Slice oranges and apples with skins; chop celery. Combine the fruit and celery; fill the ducks with as much of this mixture as they will hold. Pour 1 tablespoon of sherry in each duck. Rub skins with a mixture of bacon fat and butter. Roast in a 250 to 300°F oven; baste frequently with pan drippings until juices in body cavity are clean, about 45 to 60 minutes. Discard stuffing. Serve with wild rice and currant jelly. Serves 6 to 8.

BARBECUED WILD DUCK
MID-ATLANTIC

6 *half breasts from 3 large*   1½ *teaspoons Worcestershire*
   wild ducks   *sauce*
1 *oz. butter, melted*   6 *teaspoons lemon juice*
¾ *pt tomato ketchup*

Combine all the ingredients. Grill duck breasts until brown,
about 20 minutes, basting with the sauce. Wild duck is eaten
rare, when juice runs red. Serves 6.

SMOTHERED WILD DUCK
SOUTHWEST

1 *duck, cleaned*   2 *oz. flour*
1 *teaspoon salt*   4 *oz. bacon fat*
¼ *teaspoon white pepper*   8 *fl. oz. milk*

Cut duck into 6 or 7 pieces. Season with salt and pepper and
roll in flour. Fry slowly in hot bacon fat until brown on both
sides, about 30 minutes. Turn only once. Add the milk and
cover the pan tightly. Simmer slowly until tender, about 1
hour. Serves 3 to 4.

WILD GOOSE WITH APRICOT STUFFING
MIDWEST

1 *young wild goose (or domestic*   4 *oz. chopped tart apple*
   fowl)   4 *oz. chopped dried apricots*
1 *teaspoon lemon juice*   3 *oz. soft bread crumbs*
2 *teaspoons salt*   ½ *teaspoon salt*
½ *teaspoon pepper*   ⅛ *teaspoon pepper*
2 *oz. butter*   6 *slices bacon*
1 *oz. chopped onion*   2 *oz. bacon drippings*

Sprinkle goose inside and out with lemon juice, 2 teaspoons salt and $\frac{1}{2}$ teaspoon pepper. Melt butter in a large saucepan. Add onion and cook until tender. Stir in apples, apricots, bread crumbs, and remaining salt and pepper. Spoon the stuffing lightly into the cavity. Close opening. Cover breast with bacon slices and cheese cloth that has been soaked in bacon drippings. Place goose, breast side up, on a rack in a roasting pan. Roast in a pre-heated 325 °F oven for $2\frac{1}{2}$ to 3 hours. Baste frequently with pan drippings. For an older goose, pour one cup of water into the pan and cover during the last hour of cooking.

Duck, Chicken and Turkey

BRUNSWICK STEW
MOUNTAIN

1 *large stewing chicken*
1 *lb. veal breast*
3¼ *pts water*
8 *oz. diced raw potatoes*
2 *lb. whole grain corn (scraped from cooked cobs or canned)*
1 *lb. fresh or frozen lima beans*

4 *oz. chopped onion*
8 *whole tomatoes, sliced*
1 *teaspoon salt*
¼ *teaspoon pepper*
2 *drops tabasco sauce*
4 *drops Worcestershire sauce*
4 *oz. butter*

Stew chicken and veal together until chicken is falling from bones. Shred chicken and veal, discarding skin and fat and gristle. Return meat to broth, continue to simmer, skimming occasionally, for 2 hours. Cook potatoes in water until done. Combine vegetables with meat in broth and simmer 4 hours, until rather thick. Season with salt, pepper, tabasco sauce, Worcestershire sauce. Add butter. Serves 10.

BROILED CHICKEN
NEW ENGLAND

8 *fl. oz. vinegar (or lemon juice)*
8 *fl. oz. water*

6 *chicken halves (¾ lb. each)*
4 *oz. melted butter*

Mix all ingredients except chicken. Grill chicken very slowly (for at least 45 minutes), basting constantly with mixture. Serves 6.

CHICKEN LUAU
HAWAIIAN

4 *lb. chicken, jointed and cut*   2 *bunches luau (taro leaves) or*
   in small pieces   *fresh spinach leaves*
3 *tablespoons salt*   1¼ *pts coconut milk**

Place pieces of chicken in large pan; cover with hot water; add salt. Bring to a boil, and simmer until tender. Wash luau leaves thoroughly; remove stem and fibrous part of veins. Place in separate covered saucepan; add 1 cup water and cook until wilted. Drain, add fresh water and continue cooking. Drain, add water again, cook until tender; drain. Draw a knife through luau leaves or spinach to cut into small pieces. Add coconut milk. Place chicken in serving dish with 2 cups hot broth (with the excess fat removed), add luau and coconut milk to chicken and serve hot.

* If fresh coconut milk is absolutely unobtainable, use fresh scalded milk.

CHICKEN PIE
ALL AMERICAN

FILLING

1½ *oz. chicken fat, butter or*   ⅛ *teaspoon pepper*
   margarine   ¼ *teaspoon poultry seasoning, if*
1 *oz. flour*   *desired*
½ *pt chicken broth*   ½ *lb. cooked chicken, diced*
8 *fl. oz. milk*   ½ *lb. cooked peas and carrots*
1½ *teaspoons salt*

PASTRY FOR TOP CRUST

4 *oz. flour*   2½ *oz. shortening*
¾ *teaspoon baking powder*   2⅓ *to* 3 *tablespoons water*
½ *teaspoon salt*

Melt fat for the filling in a saucepan; blend in flour. Add broth, milk and seasonings. Cook, stirring constantly until thickened. Add chicken and vegetables; heat thoroughly. For the pastry, mix flour with baking powder and salt. Mix in fat until mixture is crumbly. Add a little water at a time blending lightly. Dough should be just moist enough to cling together when pressed into a ball. Roll dough on a lightly floured surface; shape to fit top of 9- or 10-inch pie dish. Make a few small slits near centre. Pour filling into pie dish; top with pastry. Bake at 400°F (hot oven) for 30 minutes or until browned. Serves 6.

CHICKEN SALAD
MIDWEST

1 *lb. cooked chicken, coarsely diced*
3 *tablespoons mayonnaise*
1 *oz. chopped celery*
1 *oz. chopped green pepper*
1 *dessertspoon chopped sweet pickle*

2 *tablespoons grated onion*
1 *teaspoon salt*
¼ *teaspoon white pepper*
1 *tablespoon chopped parsley*
crisp lettuce leaves

Combine all the ingredients except the parsley and the lettuce in a bowl. Chill in the refrigerator for 2 hours. Form mixture into loose mounds in lettuce leaf cups. Sprinkle with parsley. Makes 4 servings.

CHICKEN À LA KING
MID-ATLANTIC

1 *lb. cooked chicken*	2 *tablespoons flour*
1 *oz. butter*	¼ *teaspoon grated nutmeg*
1 *oz. chopped onion*	4 *fl. oz. milk*
1 *oz. chopped green pepper*	1 *teaspoon salt*
1 *oz. chopped pimento* or *chopped sweet red pepper*	½ *teaspoon white pepper*
	2 *tablespoons sherry*

Cut chicken into bite-size pieces, removing the skin and gristle. Melt butter in a heavy-bottomed saucepan. Sauté vegetables in butter until transparent, but not brown. Make a white roux with the flour. Add nutmeg and milk, stirring until smooth. Cook mixture for 15 minutes. Add chicken and seasoning to sauce. Cook 10 minutes. Serve in a vol-au-vent or over rice. Just before serving, sprinkle with sherry. Serves 6.

BRAISED CHICKEN WITH VEGETABLES
ALL AMERICAN

2 *oz. flour*	6 *fl. oz. hot water*
1 *teaspoon salt*	½ *teaspoon salt*
¼ *teaspoon pepper*	6 *oz. sliced carrots*
1 3-*lb. ready to cook chicken, jointed*	12 *oz. sliced celery*
3 *tablespoons fat or oil*	3 *oz. finely chopped onion*
	3 *oz. chopped green pepper*

Combine flour, 1 teaspoon salt with pepper. Coat chicken pieces with mixture. Brown chicken in hot fat in large frying pan. Drain excess fat from pan. Add water and ½ teaspoon salt. Cover tightly and simmer 45 minutes to 1 hour, or until chicken is almost tender. Add vegetables and cook 20 to 30 minutes longer, or until vegetables are tender. Serves 6.

Recipes

COUNTRY CAPTAIN
SOUTH

1 *chicken, about 3 lb.*
3 *tablespoons flour*
½ *teaspoon salt*
¼ *teaspoon white pepper*
2 *oz. lard*
4 *oz. finely chopped onion*
4 *oz. finely chopped green pepper*
½ *teaspoon chopped garlic*
5 *tomatoes, peeled, seeded and chopped*

2 *teaspoons curry powder*
1 *teaspoon salt*
½ *teaspoon white pepper*
½ *teaspoon powdered thyme*
½ *teaspoon chopped parsley*
8 *oz. cooked rice*
2 *oz. blanched almonds*
3 *tablespoons currants*

Joint chicken and skin it. Combine flour, salt and white pepper in a dish. Dredge chicken in flour mixture. Melt lard in a heavy frying pan. Fry chicken in hot lard; remove after 5 minutes and keep warm. Sauté vegetables in the same lard. Add seasonings and cook over a very low heat for 10 minutes. Place chicken in a heavy roaster or casserole. Pour vegetable mixture over. Cover well; cook in a pre-heated 350°F oven until chicken is done, about 45 minutes. Place chicken on platter with sauce. Surround with rice; scatter almonds and currants over. Serves 4 to 6.

FRIED CHICKEN
MID-ATLANTIC

1 *2½-lb. chicken*
1 *egg yolk*
4 *fl. oz. buttermilk*
1 *oz. soft bread crumbs*

2 *oz. flour*
2 *teaspoons salt*
1 *teaspoon paprika*
deep fat for frying

Combine egg and milk. Combine crumbs, flour and seasonings. Dip chicken in egg mixture then in crumbs. Dry on rack for a few minutes and deep fry in 350 °F fat until brown and tender, about 15 minutes. Drain in absorbent paper. Serves 4.

HOME-MADE NOODLES WITH CHICKEN
ALL AMERICAN

4 oz. flour
1 egg or ¼ cup egg yolks, slightly beaten
1 tablespoon single cream
1½ teaspoons salt
¾ teaspoon poultry seasoning

pepper as desired
2 pts chicken broth
12 oz. cubed cooked chicken
paprika
parsley

Combine first three ingredients thoroughly; form into a ball. Do not knead. Divide into two parts. Roll each part on lightly floured surface until paper thin. Allow dough to dry 5 to 10 minutes. With a thin sharp knife, cut dough into strips of desired width and length. Add seasonings to broth; bring to a boil. Add noodles; boil 9 to 12 minutes, or until tender. Add chicken; continue cooking until chicken is hot. Sprinkle with paprika and garnish with parsley. Serves 6.

POLLO GUISADO
SOUTHWEST

1 3-lb. chicken
1 oz. bacon fat
4 oz. chopped, seeded, peeled tomatoes
2 oz. chopped onions

1 teaspoon chopped green chilli pepper
½ teaspoon chopped garlic
2 oz. sliced mushrooms

Joint the chicken. Brown the pieces in fat in frying pan. Add all the chopped vegetables except the mushrooms.

Simmer for 15 minutes. Add the mushrooms and slowly cook for 30 minutes, or until chicken is tender. Serves 4 to 6.

SMOTHERED CHICKEN
MOUNTAIN

6 *day-old biscuits (see p. 251)*   ½ *teaspoon pepper*
2½ *lb. chicken, jointed*   1 *tablespoon bacon fat*
½ *pt milk*
1 *teaspoon salt*

Toast biscuits. Place chicken in a baking dish, surround with biscuits. Pour milk, seasonings and fat over chicken. Cover dish; bake 350°F oven for 1 hour. Baste frequently during cooking with milk mixture. If necessary, add additional hot milk so that some gravy will form.

SOUTHERN FRIED CHICKEN
SOUTH

1 3-*lb. chicken*   2 *oz. flour*
¾ *pt cream*   1 *lb. butter*
2 *tablespoons coarsely ground*   1 *lb. lard*
   black pepper

Joint the chicken. Soak overnight in cream and black pepper. Dip chicken pieces in flour. This can be done in a paper bag, shaken like a cocktail shaker, with flour and a few pieces of chicken at the time. Deep fry in melted lard and butter at about 350°F until done, about 20 minutes.

ROAST TURKEY WITH BARBECUE SAUCE
SOUTHWEST

1 8-*lb. turkey*	6 *oz. melted butter*
1 *tablespoon salt*	1 *teaspoon salt*
4 *oz. coarsely chopped onion*	½ *teaspoon pepper*
handful celery leaves	

Rub cavity of the bird with 1 tablespoon salt; stuff with celery leaves and onion. Truss. Brush outside of bird with some melted butter. Sprinkle with salt and pepper. Place on rack in a roasting pan; roast in a pre-heated 325 °F oven until tender, about 2½ hours. Brush with butter, and then with drippings. Thirty minutes before cooking is completed, combine some pan drippings with hot barbecue sauce (recipe below) and baste almost constantly during last 30 minutes of cooking.

Barbecue Sauce

8 *fl. oz. ketchup*	1 *tablespoon sugar*
8 *fl. oz. water*	1 *teaspoon salt*
2 *fl. oz. vinegar*	2 *or* 3 *drops red pepper sauce*
1 *tablespoon Worcestershire sauce*	

Combine all the ingredients in a saucepan. Heat mixture to boiling and simmer for 30 minutes.

TURKEY-NOODLE BAKE
ALL AMERICAN

4 oz. noodles
1 oz. flour
¾ pt mushroom liquid and water
2 chicken bouillon cubes
¼ teaspoon salt
pepper, as desired
½ teaspoon poultry seasoning
1 tablespoon chopped pimento

4 oz. can mushroom stems and
    pieces, drained, chopped
½ lb. cooked turkey, cubed
3 oz. shredded sharp processed
    cheese
1½ oz. fine dry bread crumbs
1 tablespoon butter or mar-
    garine

Cook noodles, and drain. In a saucepan, blend flour with a little of the liquid to make a paste. Gradually stir in remaining liquid. Add bouillon cubes and seasonings. Bring to a boil, stirring constantly. Reduce heat to simmer; cook 1 minute longer, stirring as needed. Add pimento and mushrooms to sauce. In a 3-pint casserole, place half the noodles and half the turkey in layers. Cover with half the sauce. Repeat layers. Top with cheese; sprinkle with breadcrumbs; dot with fat. Bake uncovered in a 350°F oven 30 to 40 minutes or until bubbly and browned.

DIAMOND HEAD DUCK
HAWAIIAN

1 duck
2 whole oranges
rum (see recipe)

1 tablespoon honey
sliced orange to garnish
½ teaspoon salt

Clean the duck thoroughly and dry the inside. Marinate one peeled orange in rum for one or two hours. Stuff the duck with the whole marinated orange and sew up. Duck should be pricked with a fork in several places to allow melted fat to escape. Spit and cook slowly on an electric rotisserie, or roast in oven. Baste frequently with a sauce made of the juice of 1 orange, 1 tablespoon of honey, $\frac{1}{2}$ teaspoon salt and 2 tablespoons of rum. Serve on a platter, garnished with orange slices. The trick in preparing this dish is to adjust the heat so that the duck takes on an appetizing, golden glaze at the exact time when all or most of the fat has been cooked out, but the meat remains juicy.

Vegetables

BOSTON BAKED BEANS
NEW ENGLAND

1 *lb. dried pea beans*
¼ *lb. lean salt pork*
¾ *pt water*
4–8 *oz. maple syrup*

1 *medium onion*
1 *teaspoon salt*
1 *teaspoon dry mustard*

Soak beans overnight. The next day, start in cold water and cook, covered, until they start to burst, about 40 minutes. Drain. Add pork (if pork is highly cured, soak in water 2 hours), water, syrup, salt and remaining ingredients to beans in heavy earthenware pot. Cover. Bake in a 300–325 °F oven for about 3 hours. Add additional water if necessary to keep beans moist. Additional syrup can be sprinkled on beans before serving. Serves 6–8.

COWBOY BEANS
WEST

12 *oz. dried red beans*
2½ *pts water*
½ *lb. bacon in piece*
¾ *pt chilli sauce or ketchup*

2 *oz. brown sugar*
2 *tablespoons dark corn syrup*
1 *large onion, thickly sliced*

Bring water to a boil in a heavy pot. Add beans and boil for 2 minutes. Remove from heat and let soak for 1 hour. Cut slab bacon to rind, but not through, in 4 or 5 slices. Combine all ingredients in pot. Bring to a boil rapidly. Tightly cover and simmer, until beans are done, about 3½ hours.

HARVARD BEETS
NEW ENGLAND

2½ oz. brown sugar
2 fl. oz. cider vinegar
2 fl. oz. water

1 teaspoon cornflour
1 lb. cooked beetroot, diced
2 tablespoons bacon fat

Combine sugar, vinegar and water (if canned beets are used, substitute beet liquid for water). Bring to a boil and cook 5 minutes. Thicken with cornflour dissolved in a little water. Add beets, cook over low heat for 30 minutes. Add bacon fat, boil 1 minute and serve. Serves 4.

CORN PUDDING
SOUTH

1 lb. corn, cut from cob (or drained canned corn)
3 eggs, lightly beaten
2 teaspoons sugar

1½ teaspoons salt
⅛ teaspoon ground black pepper
¾ pt milk
1 oz. butter

Mix corn, eggs, sugar and seasonings together in a bowl. Heat milk in a saucepan with butter until butter is melted. Add to egg mixture and stir. Pour into a casserole. Poach by setting pan into a pan of hot water in a pre-heated 350 °F oven until custard is set, about 1 hour. Serves 6.

COLACHE
SOUTHWEST

1 *oz. butter*
1 *oz. grated onion*
3 *cups summer squash, cut in ⅛-inch slices*
4 *oz. fresh corn, scraped from the cob*
4 *oz. diced, seeded, peeled tomatoes*

2 *teaspoons salt*
½ *teaspoon sugar*
½ *teaspoon ground marjoram*
¼ *teaspoon black pepper*
⅛ *teaspoon ground cumin*

Melt the butter in a saucepan. Add the grated onion. Add vegetables and seasonings. Cover the pan; cook over low heat until well combined, about 25 minutes. Serves 6.

GREEN BEANS
MOUNTAIN

½ *lb. smoked bacon (dry cured)*
1½ *pts water*
2 *lb. fresh green beans (string beans)*

1 *teaspoon sugar*
¼ *dried red pepper pod*
¼ *teaspoon white pepper*
salt

Boil bacon in a large pan with water until half-cooked, 30 to 40 minutes. Cut beans into 1-inch pieces. Add beans, sugar and red pepper to bacon. Cover with additional water if necessary. Simmer 4 hours, adding enough water to keep beans from sticking. After 3 hours adjust seasonings by adding salt and pepper. Finish cooking beans over low heat until broth is almost gone.

HUNGARIAN CABBAGE
ALL AMERICAN

2 *slices bacon*
1 *lb. coarsely shredded cabbage*
¾ *teaspoon salt*

pepper, as desired
2 *tablespoons vinegar*
2 *tablespoons water*

Fry bacon until crisp; remove from pan. Add remaining ingredients to fat in pan. Cover tightly and cook over low heat, stirring occasionally for 20 to 25 minutes. Cabbage should be tender but crisp. Crumble bacon over top before serving. Serves 6.

LIMA BEAN CREOLE
ALL AMERICAN

2 *packages* (10 *oz. each*) *frozen*
  lima beans
6 *slices bacon*
1 *oz. finely chopped onion*
2 *tablespoons chopped green*
  pepper

½ *teaspoon salt*
pepper, as desired
1 *lb. cooked or canned tomatoes*

Cook beans as directed on package; drain. Fry bacon; drain on absorbent paper. In 2 tablespoons bacon drippings, brown onion and green pepper. Crumble bacon. Add browned onion and green pepper, bacon, seasonings, and tomatoes to beans. Cover and simmer gently 15 minutes. Serves 6.

JAGESEE
NEW ENGLAND

2 lb. dry small lima beans, or
   flageolet
½ lb. salt pork (1 piece) or bacon
   (if very salted, wash and
   drain)
8 oz. onion, chopped

12 oz. long-grain rice
2 oz. celery, chopped
2 oz. green pepper, chopped
3 tablespoons tomato ketchup
2 tablespoons red sweet peppers,
   or pimento, chopped

Soak beans overnight. The next day wash in several waters.
Fry piece of salt pork in a very heavy pan until it is well
browned all over. Remove. Add onion to rendered fat and
brown thoroughly. Combine all ingredients in a heavy iron
pot and add boiling water to cover. Cook very slowly for 7
hours over low heat, adding more boiling water if beans
become dry. Serves 12.

KARTOFFEL PFANNKUCHEN
PENNSYLVANIA DUTCH

¾ lb. freshly grated potatoes
2 well-beaten eggs
1½ tablespoons flour

⅛ teaspoon baking powder
1 teaspoon salt

Add eggs to grated potatoes and mix together. Stir in remaining ingredients. Drop from spoon into well-greased pan and
brown on both sides. Serve with apple sauce. Makes 15 3-
inch pancakes.

MAWUE-CHOUX
CREOLE

1 *dozen ears fresh corn*	1 *teaspoon salt*
2 *oz. onion, chopped*	$\frac{1}{4}$ *teaspoon red pepper*
1$\frac{1}{2}$ *oz. sweet green pepper,*	2 *tablespoons cooking oil*
chopped	

Cut the corn off the cob, slicing first across the tops of kernels, then cutting balance of corn from cob. Scrape cob well to get milk; combine corn, milk, onion, pepper and seasonings. Heat oil in a heavy-bottomed pan. Add corn mixture, and cook over high heat for 20 minutes, stirring constantly. Reduce the heat, cover the pan, and simmer corn for 5 minutes longer. Serves 6.

BOILED OKRA
CREOLE

1$\frac{1}{2}$ *lb. okra*	1 *tablespoon vinegar*
1$\frac{1}{4}$ *pts boiling water*	3 *tablespoons butter*
$\frac{1}{2}$ *teaspoon salt*	$\frac{1}{4}$ *teaspoon pepper*

Choose young tender crisp pods of okra about 2 to 4 inches in length. Remove the stems from the pods. Cut them in $\frac{1}{2}$-inch slices. Put boiling water and salt in a saucepan. Add okra and vinegar and cook until pods are tender, about 15 minutes. Drain the cooked okra. Add butter and season with salt. Serves 6.

Recipes

FRIED OKRA
MOUNTAIN

1 *lb. okra pods*
5 *oz. cornmeal*
1 *teaspoon salt*

½ *teaspoon black pepper*
½ *cup bacon fat*

Wash okra and slice off ends. Slice in ½-inch pieces. Roll in cornmeal and seasonings. Brown quickly in hot fat.

POTATO PATTIES
ALL AMERICAN

8 *oz. seasoned mashed potatoes*
1 *egg or 2 egg yolks, slightly beaten*
1 *tablespoon finely chopped onion*

1 *tablespoon chopped green pepper*
2 *tablespoons fat or oil*

Combine all ingredients except fat; mix well. Shape into six patties. Brown well in hot fat, about 4 minutes on each side.
Note: Leftover mashed potatoes or instant mashed potatoes, prepared according to package directions, may be used in this recipe.

STUFFED BAKED POTATOES
ALL AMERICAN

6 *medium-sized baking potatoes*
1 *package (3 oz.) cream cheese, at room temperature*
½ *gill milk*

1 *teaspoon salt*
2½ *oz. butter or margarine*
paprika

Rub potatoes with a little fat if soft skins are desired. Bake in a pre-heated 425 °F oven 50 to 60 minutes, or until potato is soft when pressed. Slash tops lengthwise and crosswise. Fold back flaps, scoop out inside, and mash thoroughly. Soften cream cheese and blend in milk, salt and fat until smooth and creamy. Add cream cheese mixture gradually to hot potato, blending thoroughly. Stuff skins with potato mixture. Sprinkle with paprika. Return to oven a few minutes to brown tops. Serves 6.

HASHED BROWN POTATOES
MIDWEST

8 oz. bacon fat
8 oz. peeled, boiled potatoes, drained and diced
1 teaspoon salt

$\frac{1}{4}$ teaspoon coarsely ground black pepper
2 tablespoons melted butter

Melt the bacon fat in a heavy frying pan. Add the potatoes and sprinkle with seasonings. Form the potatoes into a round omelette shape. Press down and cook over moderate heat until bottom is browned, about 20 minutes. Shake the pan and re-form the omelette and rebrown twice. Finally turn potato omelette from pan. Glaze with melted butter.

FRIJOLES FRIJOLES REFRITOS
SOUTHWEST

1 lb. pinto beans
2½ pts water
4 tablespoons bacon fat
4 oz. chopped onion
8 oz. tomato sauce

3 teaspoons chilli powder
1 teaspoon chopped garlic
½ teaspoon crushed oregano
½ teaspoon ground cumin
¼ teaspoon coarse ground pepper

Wash beans. Soak in water overnight. Add 2 tablespoons bacon fat to beans and water and bring to a boil. Reduce heat; simmer until beans are tender, not mushy, about 2 hours. Drain, reserving liquid. Cook onion in remaining bacon fat. Add remaining ingredients and ½ cup liquid from beans. Add this mixture to beans; cover pan and allow to simmer for 2 hours. Add salt as necessary.

Frijoles Refritos

After cooling Frijoles, remove beans from surrounding liquid. Heat a small quantity of fat in a heavy pan. Heat beans and fat into a semi-dry mass.

RED BEAN PURÉE
CREOLE

1 *lb. dried red kidney beans*
1 *oz. flour*
2 *oz. bacon fat*
3 *oz. onion, chopped*
½ *teaspoon garlic, chopped*
1 *teaspoon salt*
¼ *teaspoon red pepper*
¾ *pt water*
1 *tablespoon chopped spring onion*
2 *tablespoons parsley, chopped*

Soak beans overnight in water. Drain the beans, cover with cold water in saucepan; cover the pan and simmer until beans are done. Pass the beans through a sieve, separating the skins from the pulp. Make a roux of the flour and bacon fat in a heavy pan. Add onion, garlic and spices; cook mixture 5 minutes. Add bean pulp and water to roux; simmer mixture, stirring constantly until it is the consistency of thick cream (about 30 minutes). Add spring onions and parsley. Serve bean purée with crackers. Makes 1½ quarts.

SPANISH RICE WITH CHEESE
ALL AMERICAN

3 *slices bacon*
1 *small onion, finely chopped*
1 *oz. chopped green pepper*
1 *oz. chopped celery*
8 *fl. oz. water*
½ *teaspoon salt*

6 *oz. rice*
1 *lb. cooked or canned tomatoes*
1 *teaspoon sugar*
¼ *teaspoon Worcestershire sauce*
4 *oz. shredded Cheddar cheese*

Fry bacon in a heavy 4-pint saucepan. Drain bacon on paper. In 1 tablespoon bacon drippings, lightly brown onion, green pepper, and celery. Add water and salt; bring to a boil. Stir in rice, tomatoes, sugar and Worcestershire sauce. Simmer until rice is just tender, stirring occasionally. Crumble bacon and stir into rice mixture. Sprinkle cheese over top. Cover and continue cooking over very low heat until cheese is melted, about 5 minutes. Serves 6.

NEW ORLEANS RICE
CREOLE

2 *oz. sliced onion*
2 *oz. chopped celery*
1½ *tablespoons bacon fat*
¾ *tablespoon flour*
1 *gill water*
¼ *teaspoon salt*
2 *oz. peeled, seeded tomatoes*

2 *oz. cooked peas*
½ *tablespoon vinegar*
¼ *teaspoon sugar*
2 *oz. cooked peeled and cleaned shrimps*
½ *tablespoon chilli powder*
8 *oz. rice, boiled*

Sauté the onions and celery in fat in a heavy-bottomed pan until browned. Stir in the flour and slowly add the water and salt. Simmer mixture for 15 minutes, stirring it frequently.

Add tomatoes, peas, vinegar and sugar to mixture. Stir in the shrimps and chilli powder, and continue cooking sauce for 10 minutes. Place rice in serving dish and pour sauce mixture over it. Serves 4.

EJOTES (STRING BEANS)
SOUTHWEST

1 *lb. strung, broken string beans*
2 *tablespoons olive oil*
2 *oz. chopped onion*
¼ *teaspoon chopped garlic*
1 *oz. chopped green chilli peppers*

1 *teaspoon vinegar*
1 *teaspoon salt*
¼ *teaspoon white pepper*

Wash the string beans and drain. Heat olive oil in a frying pan and sauté the onion and garlic for one minute. Add the beans and coat them well with the mixture. Add the other vegetables and seasonings. Simmer the covered pan until beans are tender, about 20 minutes.

STUFFED SWEET POTATOES
SOUTH

6 *large even sweet potatoes*
2 *oz. bacon drippings*
10 *rashers bacon*
2 *tablespoons chopped onion*

1 *oz. butter*
½ *teaspoon salt*
2 *tablespoons chopped parsley*

Heat oven to 450 °F. Scrub and dry sweet potatoes. Rub each with a small amount of bacon drippings. Arrange potatoes on a baking sheet. Bake until tender, about 35 minutes. In a frying pan, fry bacon until crisp; drain. Reserve 6 strips of bacon for garnish and crumble the rest into a mixing bowl.

204

Sauté onion in remaining bacon drippings. Remove tops from potatoes by making a lengthwise cut. Scoop out potato, taking care not to tear jackets. Combine scooped-out potatoes with crumbled bacon, sautéd onion, butter and salt. Beat until light and fluffy. Fill jackets with the fluffy potatoes and return to oven until hot and slightly brown, about 10 minutes. Sprinkle with chopped parsley; garnish with reserved bacon slices. Serves 6.

GRILLED TOMATOES
ALL AMERICAN

3 *large or 6 small ripe tomatoes*
salt and pepper, as desired
2 *teaspoons butter or margarine*

2 *tablespoons fine dry bread crumbs*

Wash tomatoes; cut off stem ends. Cut large tomatoes in 1-inch slices; cut small tomatoes in half crosswise. Place cut side up on a grill pan rack. Sprinkle with salt and pepper. Dot each slice with fat and sprinkle with bread crumbs. Grill until tomatoes are soft and crumbs lightly browned, 5 to 7 minutes. Serves 6.

FRIED GREEN TOMATOES
MOUNTAIN

8 *medium-sized unripe tomatoes*
1 *teaspoon salt*
1 *teaspoon sugar*

$\frac{1}{2}$ *teaspoon white pepper*
5 *oz. cornmeal*
4 *oz. bacon drippings*

Slice tomatoes in $\frac{1}{4}$-inch thick slices. Discard ends. Sprinkle slices with seasonings and dip in cornmeal. Heat fat in a heavy pan; add tomatoes. Reduce heat and brown on one side for about 10 minutes. Serves 4.

SCALLOPED TOMATOES
MIDWEST

2 oz. fresh bread crumbs
6 tomatoes, peeled, seeded and sliced
1 teaspoon sugar
$\frac{1}{2}$ teaspoon salt
$\frac{1}{8}$ teaspoon pepper
$\frac{1}{8}$ teaspoon nutmeg
6 oz. butter

Layer the inside of a $1\frac{1}{2}$-quart greased casserole with bread crumbs. Add half the tomatoes. Cover with half the remaining bread crumbs. Add remaining tomatoes and seasoning. Dot with butter. Cover with remaining crumbs; dot with remaining butter. Bake in a moderate pre-heated 350 °F oven until top is browned and bubbly, about 30 minutes.

MASHED TURNIPS
MOUNTAIN

8 oz. sliced peeled turnips
8 oz. chopped salt pork
$\frac{3}{4}$ pt water
1 teaspoon pepper
4 tablespoons sugar
4 tablespoons butter

Cover turnip slices with water, add salt pork and cook over low heat until water is entirely gone. Mash with fork; return to heat and season with pepper, sugar and butter.

TURNIP GREENS
MOUNTAIN

2 lb. turnip greens
$\frac{1}{2}$ lb. jowl bacon, washed
4 oz. chopped onions
3 pts water
4 oz. sliced onions

Wash greens thoroughly and remove spotted leaves and tough stems. Cook bacon and chopped onions together with water in a saucepan until meat is tender, about 3 hours. Add turnip greens and simmer until tender, about 2 hours. Serve in a large bowl with plenty of turnip-green water. Put sliced onions on top. Serves 4 to 6.

WILD RICE
WEST

8 oz. wild rice   1 tablespoon salt
2 pts water

Wash rice thoroughly in a fine sieve under running water, until the water runs clear. Combine rice, water and salt in a large pan. Bring to a slow rolling boil and boil until all the kernels are light and fluffy, about 1 hour. Drain in colander. Do not stir. Cover with a towel and set colander over boiling water until ready to use. Makes 3 to 4 cups.

VEGETABLES OAHU
HAWAIIAN

carrots   tomato
beans   turnips
leeks   onion
cauliflower   vegetable oil for sautéing
green pepper

Slice the carrots, leeks, turnips and green peppers lengthwise and thin. Cauliflower and tomato should be diced small. Add enough onion to season to taste. Put enough vegetable oil in a large frying pan to cover the bottom well and heat until very hot. Add vegetable ingredients and sauté over high flame until the vegetables are tender, but not over-cooked. (They should be crunchy, not soggy.)

Salads

AVOCADO MOULDED SALAD
FARWEST

½ oz. unflavoured gelatine
4 oz. warm water
1 avocado (passed through a food mill)
8 oz. sour cream
1 tablespoon lemon juice

2 tablespoons grated onion
1 teaspoon sugar
½ teaspoon red pepper sauce
¼ teaspoon salt
½ an avocado, sliced for garnish
crisp lettuce leaves for garnish

Dissolve the gelatine in the warm water. Pour it into a large bowl. Add all the ingredients except the garnishes and beat until smooth. Chill this avocado mixture until almost firm. Remove from refrigerator and beat to incorporate some air. Pour the mixture into a 6-cup mould and chill until firm. Garnish the mould with lettuce and avocado slices. Serves 4.

SUNSHINE COLE SLAW
WEST

1 lb. shredded cabbage
6 oz. shredded carrots
1 oz. finely sliced green pepper

½ gill mayonnaise
1 tablespoon lemon juice
1 teaspoon celery seed

Combine vegetables in a large bowl. Add mayonnaise, lemon juice and celery seed. Toss until vegetables are coated.

Place in refrigerator to allow flavour to develop (about 3 hours). Serves 6.

COLE SLAW
MID-ATLANTIC

1½ teaspoons salt
½ teaspoon dry mustard
white pepper, as desired
1½ oz. sugar
2 tablespoons lemon juice
1 tablespoon tarragon vinegar
½ gill single cream
12 oz. coarsely shredded cabbage

1 oz. finely chopped green pepper
1 tablespoon chopped pimento
2 oz. finely chopped celery
2 tablespoons finely chopped onion

Thoroughly mix all ingredients except vegetables. Combine vegetables in a bowl. Mix well. Gently stir in the dressing. Chill before serving. Serves 6.

CREAMY FRUIT SALAD
ALL AMERICAN

1 package (3 oz.) cream cheese
1 tablespoon syrup from canned mandarin oranges
1 can (11 oz.) mandarin orange sections, drained
1 can (13½ oz.) pineapple tidbits, drained

4 oz. miniature marshmallows
2 oz. halved, drained maraschino cherries
lettuce

Beat cream cheese with liquid from mandarin oranges until creamy. Add oranges, pineapple and marshmallows; combine gently but thoroughly. Lightly fold in cherries. Chill. Serve in lettuce cups. Serves 6.

HOT GREEN SALAD
MIDWEST

5 *tablespoons bacon drippings*
1 *tablespoon grated onion*
4 *oz. chopped washed spinach*
1 *head chopped washed soft lettuce leaves*

½ *teaspoon ground black pepper*
½ *teaspoon salt*
1 *tablespoon cider vinegar*

Heat bacon fat in a frying pan. Add onion. Combine chopped spinach and lettuce, salt and pepper with the onion in the frying pan. Heat until wilted. Sprinkle with vinegar; serve immediately. Serves 4.

LUNCHEON CHEF SALAD BOWL
ALL AMERICAN

2 *medium heads lettuce*
8 *radishes, thinly sliced*
4 *spring onions, with tops, thinly sliced*
3 *large ripe tomatoes, cut into 8 wedges each*

1 *lb. cooked ham cut into 1-inch cubes*
8 *oz. coarsely shredded Swiss cheese*
croûtons
salad dressing

Wash and drain lettuce. Reserve outer lettuce leaves; tear remaining lettuce into bite-size pieces. Combine torn lettuce, radishes and spring onions; toss lightly. Line 6 individual salad bowls with lettuce leaves. For each salad, use 2 cups lettuce mixture and top with 4 tomato wedges, ½ cup ham cubes, and ⅓ cup shredded cheese. Top with croûtons. Serve with dressing of your choice. Makes 6 servings.

SOUFFLÉ MEAT SALAD
ALL AMERICAN

½ oz. gelatine
juice of 1 lemon
8 fl. oz. boiling water
4 fl. oz. cold water
4 fl. oz. salad dressing
2 tablespoons vinegar
¼ teaspoon salt

pepper, as desired
2 oz. chopped celery
1 tablespoon chopped parsley
1 tablespoon grated onion
8 oz. chopped cooked meat
salad greens

Dissolve gelatine in boiling water. Add cold water, salad dressing, juice of lemon, vinegar, salt and pepper. Beat until smooth. Chill until slightly thickened. Whip until fluffy. Fold in celery, parsley, onion and meat. Pour into a 1-quart mould. Chill until firm. Unmould on salad greens. Makes 6 servings.

ORANGE AND CARROT
GELATINE SALAD
MIDWEST

2 dessertspoons gelatine
4 fl. oz. cold water
¾ pt boiling water
8 fl. oz. orange juice and pulp
  (squeeze without straining)

2 tablespoons tarragon vinegar
1 tablespoon lemon juice
1 tablespoon sugar
½ teaspoon salt
4 oz. grated raw carrots

Soak gelatine in cold water for 5 minutes. Add to boiling water, orange juice, vinegar, lemon juice, sugar and salt. Chill slowly; when partly jellied, stir in carrots. Pour into individual moulds; allow to set in the refrigerator. Turn out on lettuce and serve with mayonnaise dressing.

MOULDED PINEAPPLE-CARROT SALAD
ALL AMERICAN

½ oz. gelatine made up with
    juice of 2 lemons, pineapple
    syrup and water to 1 pt
4 oz. shredded raw carrots
1 can (10½ oz.) crushed pine-
    apple, drained

1 oz. raisins
lettuce
mayonnaise

Prepare gelatine using pineapple syrup as part of the liquid.
Chill until mixture is slightly thickened. Fold in carrots,
pineapple, and raisins; pour into a 1-quart mould. Chill until
firm. Serve on lettuce; top with mayonnaise if desired.
Serves 6.

POTATO SALAD
MID-ATLANTIC

8 medium-sized potatoes
1½ teaspoons salt
2 oz. onion, sliced
1 oz. celery, chopped
1 oz. green pepper, chopped

4 hard-boiled eggs, chopped
8 fl. oz. mayonnaise
2 teaspoons vinegar
½ teaspoon prepared mustard

Boil potatoes in jackets. Peel, cut in quarters then in ¼-inch
slices. Sprinkle with salt. Mix in bowl with onion, celery, green
pepper and egg. Combine mayonnaise, vinegar and mustard.
Add to potatoes. Chill 5 hours. Serves 6.

Can be garnished with tomato wedges and hard-boiled egg
quarters.

STUFFED PRUNE SALAD
ALL AMERICAN

4 oz. creamed cottage cheese
1 to 2 tablespoons milk, if needed
1 to 2 teaspoons grated orange rind, as desired

1 oz. chopped peanuts
¼ teaspoon salt (if peanuts are unsalted)
18 chilled, pitted, cooked prunes
salad greens

If cottage cheese is dry, soften it with milk. Mix in orange rind, 2 tablespoons peanuts and salt; stuff into prunes. Arrange prunes on salad greens; sprinkle with rest of peanuts. Serves 6.

PURSLANE SALAD
SOUTHWEST

2 lb. purslane
1¼ pts boiling water
1 teaspoon salt
1 oz. grated onion
4 tablespoons olive oil

1 tablespoon good vinegar
½ teaspoon salt
¼ teaspoon grated garlic
⅛ teaspoon white pepper

Wash purslane. Remove stems. Add 1 teaspoon salt to the boiling water and blanch the purslane. Drain well. Chop the purslane coarsely and place in a salad bowl. Mix together remaining ingredients with purslane. Chill for 3 hours. Makes 4 servings.

Sauces, Dips and Dressings

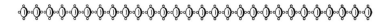

BUL KOGI BARBECUE SAUCE
HAWAIIAN

2 oz. soy sauce
1 oz. sugar
1 tablespoon vegetable oil
½ clove garlic, minced

2 stalks scallions, chopped
½ teaspoon monosodium gluta-
mate

Combine ingredients and stir until they are blended. Serve
with chicken, fish, etc.

SAUCE REMOULADE CREOLE
CREOLE

4 hard-boiled egg yolks
1 tablespoon lemon juice
½ teaspoon Dijon-style mustard
2 tablespoons olive oil
1 raw egg yolk

½ tablespoon chopped capers
½ teaspoon horseradish
½ teaspoon chopped garlic
⅛ teaspoon cayenne

Mash hard-boiled egg yolks in bowl. Combine with lemon
juice and prepared mustards. Slowly add olive oil as though
making mayonnaise. Add raw egg yolk, lightly beating in the
same fashion, continuing to make sauce like mayonnaise. Add
capers, horseradish, garlic and cayenne to mixture. Serve with
shrimps, salads, etc.

TARTAR SAUCE
ALL AMERICAN

1 *gill mayonnaise or salad oil*
1 *tablespoon chopped olives*
1 *tablespoon chopped onion*

1 *tablespoon chopped parsley*
1 *tablespoon chopped sweet pickle*

Combine all ingredients and mix well. Chill. Serve with fish.

HONEY-ORANGE SAUCE
ALL AMERICAN

5 *oz. honey*
1 *tablespoon cornflour*
1 *teaspoon grated orange rind*
4 *fl. oz. orange juice*

$\frac{1}{2}$ *gill water*
2 *tablespoons butter* or *margarine*

Combine honey, cornflour and orange rind in a heavy saucepan. Stir in orange juice and water. Bring to a boil; add fat and blend well. Cool slightly. (Sauce thickens as it cools.) Can be spooned over warm gingerbread or other desserts.

SOUR CREAM SAUCE
ALL AMERICAN

8 *oz. sour cream*
1 *tablespoon chopped fresh or frozen chives or green onion tops*

$\frac{1}{4}$ *teaspoon salt*
3 *drops Worcestershire sauce*
white pepper, as desired

Combine all ingredients thoroughly at least 2 hours before serving. Refrigerate. Serve at room temperature or slightly chilled. Can be served with broccoli or baked potatoes.

Sauces, Dips and Dressings

THE FOLLOWING SIX DRESSINGS ARE FOR SERVING WITH SALADS;

CELERY SEED DRESSING
ALL AMERICAN

2½ oz. sugar
2 tablespoons lemon juice
1 tablespoon tarragon vinegar
1½ teaspoons salt

½ teaspoon paprika
½ teaspoon dry mustard
1 teaspoon celery seed
1 gill salad oil

Thoroughly mix all ingredients except salad oil. Add the oil slowly while beating constantly with rotary or electric beater. Cover and refrigerate until used.

THOUSAND ISLAND DRESSING
ALL AMERICAN

8 fl. oz. mayonnaise
2 tablespoons sweet pickle relish
2 tablespoons chilli sauce
1 tablespoon chopped green pepper

1 tablespoon finely chopped onion
1 hard-boiled egg, finely chopped

Mix all ingredients except the egg. Gently mix in the chopped egg. Cover and refrigerate until used.

BASIC FRENCH DRESSING
ALL AMERICAN

1 gill salad oil
1 tablespoon tarragon vinegar
2 tablespoons lemon juice
1½ teaspoons salt

½ teaspoon paprika
½ teaspoon dry mustard
white pepper, as desired

217

Thoroughly mix all ingredients. Chill. Shake well just before serving.

Variations

Sweet French dressing – Increase vinegar to 2 tablespoons and add 2 ounce sugar.

Italian dressing – Use ¼ teaspoon white pepper. Add 1 ounce finely chopped onion, 1 teaspoon finely chopped garlic, 2 tablespoons sugar, 4 fluid ounces ketchup, and ½ teaspoon oregano. Refrigerate, covered, overnight to blend flavours. Strain to remove onion and garlic before serving.

ROQUEFORT CHEESE DRESSING
ALL AMERICAN

8 *oz. mayonnaise*
1 *package (4 oz.) Roquefort or blue cheese, crumbled*

2 *tablespoons single cream*
½ *teaspoon tabasco sauce*

Mix all ingredients in a bowl. Cover and refrigerate until used.

ORANGE-HONEY FRENCH DRESSING
ALL AMERICAN

2 *gills orange juice frozen concentrate*
1 *tablespoon vinegar*
2 *oz. honey*

½ *teaspoon dry mustard*
½ *teaspoon salt*
1 *gill salad oil*

Thoroughly mix all ingredients except salad oil. Slowly add the oil while beating constantly with rotary or electric beater. Cover and refrigerate until used.

WINE SALAD DRESSING
FARWEST

6 *oz. salad oil*
4 *tablespoons burgundy*
4 *tablespoons red-wine vinegar*
4 *tablespoons ketchup*
1 *tablespoon sugar*

1 *teaspoon salt*
1 *teaspoon Worcestershire sauce*
½ *teaspoon dry mustard*
½ *teaspoon grated garlic*

Combine all ingredients in a shaker. Shake mixture until well mixed. Allow it to develop overnight.

APRICOT SAUCE HONI
HAWAIIAN

½ *lb. dried apricots*
8 *fl. oz. water*
¼ *teaspoon salt*
2 *oz. sugar*

8 *fl. oz. rum*
½ *gill cider vinegar*
2 *tablespoons honey*
1 *teaspoon paprika*

Cook the dried apricots in covered saucepan until soft (about 30 minutes). Pulverize the cooked apricots in an electric blender or food mill. Add rest of ingredients and heat until smooth. This sauce will keep for months if properly refrigerated. Makes about 1 pint.

LEMON-BUTTER SAUCE
ALL AMERICAN

2 *oz. melted butter or margarine*
¾ *teaspoon salt*
¾ *teaspoon paprika*

1 *tablespoon lemon juice*
2 *teaspoons prepared horseradish*

Mix all ingredients well. Serve hot over vegetables or fish.

Recipes

SALMON SOUR CREAM DIP
FARWEST

1 *lb. canned salmon*
1 *teaspoon grated onion*
½ *teaspoon salt*
3 *drops red pepper sauce*

8 *fl. oz. sour cream*
1 *tablespoon drained red (salmon) caviar*

Drain and mash the salmon. Put salmon in a bowl and blend in onion, salt and red pepper sauce. Fold sour cream into the salmon. Chill; garnish with caviar. Serve with crackers. Makes 1 pint of dip.

GUACAMOLE
FARWEST

2 *large avocado pears, ripe*
8 *oz. mayonnaise*
1 *tablespoon lemon juice*
1 *tablespoon grated onion*

1 *teaspoon salt*
½ *teaspoon grated garlic*
½ *teaspoon white pepper*

Peel, stone and mash avocados. Add the remaining ingredients; beat until light. Serve as a dip with pieces of tostados (p. 170).

CHILLI SAUCE
SOUTHWEST

5 *chillis*
3 *large chopped, seeded tomatoes*
1 *large onion, chopped*
1 *large clove garlic, chopped*

salt and pepper
1 *teaspoon sugar*
5 *tablespoons olive oil*
2 *tablespoons wine vinegar*

Purée chillis, tomatoes, onion and garlic in electric blender. Heat 2 tablespoons oil, add purée, cook 5 minutes stirring constantly, season to taste and add sugar. Cool. Stir vinegar and remaining oil in well.

Pies and Puddings

APPLE CRISP
NEW ENGLAND

2 *lb. peeled apples, sliced*
4 *oz. sifted plain flour*

2½ *oz. brown sugar*
2½ *oz. butter*

Layer the apples in a baking dish. Combine the flour, sugar and then cut the butter in to make an even crumbly mixture. Sprinkle this over the apples. Bake in a pre-heated 350°F oven until apples are tender. Serve warm with cream or ice cream. Serves 8.

TWO-CRUST APPLE PIE
NEW ENGLAND

6 *medium-sized apples*
pastry for 9-inch 2-crust pie
7 *oz. sugar*

1 *teaspoon cinnamon*
1 *teaspoon salt*
1 *oz. butter*

Pare, core and slice apples. Line a 9-inch pie dish with pastry. Place a layer of apples on the bottom of the dish; sprinkle with a mixture of sugar, cinnamon and salt. Dot with butter. Repeat the procedure until all the ingredients are used. Cover the apples with pastry. Make a few slits in the centre of the pastry to allow the steam to escape. Seal edges of crusts

Recipes

together. Bake in a 425 °F oven for about 45 minutes or until the apples are tender and the crust is well browned.

Pastry for Two-crust Pie

8 oz. sifted flour
⅔ teaspoon salt

4 oz. shortening, chilled
6 tablespoons iced water

Sift flour and salt together in a mixing bowl. Cut shortening into flour mixture to form small crumbly balls. Add the water quickly. Chill the mixture; roll out to fit pie dish.

BUTTERMILK SHERBET
MIDWEST

¾ pt buttermilk
12 oz. drained crushed pine-apple

⅔ cup icing sugar
1 teaspoon vanilla
¼ teaspoon salt

Chill a mixing bowl that can be placed in the freezer. Blend all the ingredients in another mixing bowl thoroughly. Pour into the chilled bowl. Place in the freezer. When half-frozen, remove and beat. Continue to freeze until mixture is mushy. Serves 6.

DEEP DISH APPLE PIE
NEW ENGLAND

6 medium-sized tart apples
3½ oz. granulated sugar
4 oz. brown sugar
2 tablespoons lemon peel, grated
2 tablespoons orange peel, grated

½ teaspoon nutmeg, grated
1½ oz. butter
4 oz. pastry for 1 pie crust

Peel and core apples, cut in eighths. Layer in 9-inch-deep baking dish. Combine sugar and spices. Sprinkle on apples, dot with butter, top with thin pastry crust. Pierce pastry in decorative pattern to allow steam to escape. Bake in a 425 °F oven until the apples are soft and pastry golden, about 45 minutes. Serves 6.

APPLE PIE
ALL AMERICAN

8 *oz. pastry*
1½ *lb. pared, sliced tart apples*
5 *oz. sugar*
1 *tablespoon cornflour*

½ *teaspoon cinnamon*
1 *oz. butter or margarine, if desired*

Prepare unbaked pastry. Mix dry ingredients lightly with apples in a bowl. Put filling into pastry-lined pan. Dot with fat, if desired. Cover with pastry. Bake in a pre-heated 400 °F oven for 40 to 60 minutes or until filling bubbles and the crust is golden brown. Makes one 8-inch pie. Serves 6.

Variations
Blueberry Pie – Use 1 pound fresh blueberries instead of apples. Omit cinnamon and increase cornflour to 3 tablespoons. Sprinkle fruit with 2 tablespoons lemon juice. Bake 50 to 60 minutes.

Cherry Pie – Instead of apples, use 1 tin (1 pound) pitted red sour cherries, water pack. Do not drain. Omit cinnamon. Increase cornflour to 2 tablespoons. Add ⅛ teaspoon almond extract and a few drops of red food colouring, if desired. Bake 40 to 45 minutes.

Peach Pie – Use 1 pound fresh sliced peaches instead of apples. Use only ¼ teaspoon cinnamon. Bake 40 to 50 minutes.

Recipes

GRAHAM CRACKER CRUST
ALL AMERICAN

2½ oz. butter or margarine   6 oz. graham cracker crumbs
2 tablespoons sugar

Stir fat and sugar together in a saucepan over low heat until fat is melted. Blend in cracker crumbs. Press evenly into an 8- or 9-inch pie dish. Chill. Makes one 8- or 9-inch pie shell.

CHERRY COBBLER
ALL AMERICAN
(use recipe p. 252 adding 1 tablespoon sugar)

½ recipe sweet biscuit dough   1 can (1 lb.) pitted red sour
  (use recipe p. 252 adding   cherries, water pack
  1 tablespoon sugar)   ⅛ teaspoon almond extract
2½ oz. sugar   few drops red food colouring
2 tablespoons cornflour   ½ oz. butter or margarine

Make biscuit dough but do not roll out. Blend sugar and corn-flour in a saucepan. Gradually stir in cherries. Cook over moderate heat until thickened and clear, stirring constantly. Remove from heat. Add flavouring, food colouring, and fat. Pour into a 1½-pint casserole. Drop biscuit dough by spoonfuls on to hot cherry mixture. Bake at 425 °F 15 to 20 minutes, or until filling bubbles and topping is lightly browned. Serves 6.

CHESS PIE
SOUTH

4 oz. butter   1 teaspoon vanilla
7 oz. brown sugar   ¼ teaspoon salt
4 eggs, slightly beaten   4 oz. pecan halves
11½ fl. oz. dark corn syrup   1 9-inch unbaked pastry shell

Cream butter with sugar in a mixing bowl. Add eggs and blend well. Gradually stir in syrup, vanilla, salt and pecan halves without beating. Pour mixture into pastry shell. Bake in a 375 °F oven until mixture puffs, about 10 minutes. Then reduce heat to 350° and bake until mixture sets, about 20 more minutes.

'GRUNT'
(a type of steamed pudding)
NEW ENGLAND

7 oz. sugar	3 teaspoons baking powder
4 fl. oz. water	¼ teaspoon salt
1 lb. fruit (berries, apples, etc.)	1 tablespoon bacon fat
6 oz. plain flour, sifted	½ gill milk

Combine sugar and water, cook 5 minutes. Add fruit, cook until just soft. Butter a pudding basin, fill with prepared fruits. Sift dry ingredients, and cut in bacon fat with a pastry blender. Add milk to make a soft dough, roll out to fit over fruit. Cover the mould with buttered greaseproof paper and cloth or foil, place in boiling water to 1 inch from the top. Steam for 1 to 1½ hours, adding boiling water when necessary.

HAUPIA (COCONUT PUDDING)
HAWAIIAN

2 large coconuts	2 tablespoons cornflour
12 fl. oz. milk	pinch of salt
4 tablespoons sugar	

Grate coconut. Heat milk; pour over grated coconut meat. Allow to soak for an hour. Squeeze coconut in a kitchen towel, reserving the coconut cream extracted. Combine cornflour and half the coconut cream, sugar and salt; slowly stir in the remaining cream. Stir constantly, cooking for 5 minutes. Pour into custard cups; cool.

QUICK ICE CREAM DESSERTS
ALL AMERICAN

Pecan Balls – Toast pecans by spreading in a shallow pan and baking at 300 °F 15 to 20 minutes or until slightly browned. Cool and chop. Shape ice cream into balls. Roll balls in pecans. Place on a tray covered with wax paper and return to freezer until firm. Just before serving, top balls with hot fudge sauce.

Snowballs – Shape ice cream into balls. Roll balls in flaked coconut. Return balls to freezer as directed above.

Buttered Nut Sundae – Add 2 ounces chopped pecans or walnuts to 1 ounce melted butter or margarine in a frying pan. Toast nuts over low heat for 15 to 20 minutes, stirring as needed, until they are lightly browned. Stir in 2 ounces brown sugar, and $\frac{1}{2}$ gill water; simmer 2 minutes. Pour warm sauce over ice cream.

JOHNNY CAKE
MOUNTAIN

1 *rounded teaspoon baking soda*	2 *eggs, well beaten*
1½ *lb. corn meal*	¾ *pt sour milk*
1 *teaspoon salt*	2 *oz. melted butter*
1 *teaspoon sugar*	2 *tablespoons bacon grease*

Sift soda with 5 ounces cornmeal in a mixing bowl. Add salt and sugar. Mix eggs with milk in a bowl. Then mix in dry ingredients, adding more cornmeal to make a batter that resembles a layer cake batter. Stir in the melted butter. Grease a black iron pan with bacon fat. Turn cornmeal mixture into pan. Bake in a pre-heated 400 °F oven until brown, about 25 minutes.

LEMON CHIFFON PIE
ALL AMERICAN

1 8-*inch graham cracker crust* (*see p.* 224) *or pastry shell*	4 *fl. oz. lemon juice*
1 *tablespoon unflavoured gelatine*	½ *teaspoon grated lemon rind*
	5 *oz. sugar*
½ *gill cold water*	3 *egg whites*
3 *egg yolks*	¼ *teaspoon salt*

Prepare graham cracker crust or pastry shell. Soften gelatine in cold water. Beat egg yolks slightly. Add juice, rind and half the sugar. Cook over low heat, stirring constantly, until mixture coats the back of the spoon, 10 to 15 minutes. Add gelatine; stir until dissolved. Chill until mixture begins to thicken. Beat egg whites until foamy. Add salt and beat until soft peaks form. Slowly add remaining sugar, beating constantly until stiff. Fold into chilled mixture. Pour into crust and chill until firm. Makes one 8-inch pie, serves 6.

OATMEAL PIE
MOUNTAIN

3½ *oz. sugar*	3 *eggs*
2 *oz. butter*	½ *teaspoon vanilla*
½ *teaspoon cinnamon*	5 *oz. fine oatmeal*
¼ *teaspoon salt*	1 *oz. chopped walnuts*
1½ *oz. dark corn syrup*	1 *unbaked 9-inch pastry shell*

Cream sugar and butter together in a bowl. Add cinnamon and salt. Stir in the syrup; add eggs one at a time, stirring after each addition. Stir in vanilla, oats and walnuts. Pour into pastry shell. Bake in a pre-heated 350 °F oven for about an hour or until knife comes out clean.

OREGON TART
FAR WEST

8 *oz. butter*
7 *oz. granulated sugar*
3 *egg yolks*
5 *oz. unsifted plain flour*
5 *oz. toasted filberts, finely chopped or hazelnuts, finely chopped*
½ *teaspoon salt*

1 *lb. fresh cranberries*
4 *oz. light brown sugar*
½ *gill orange juice*
3 *teaspoons grated orange peel*
12 *filberts or hazelnuts, whole for garnish*
8 *fl. oz. sour cream*

Cream butter and granulated sugar together in a large mixing bowl until light and fluffy. Stir in egg yolks, flour, nuts and ¼ teaspoon of the salt. Mix well. Divide the dough in half and chill for 1½ hours. Meanwhile, combine cranberries, brown sugar, juice, orange peel and remaining ¼ teaspoon of salt in a pan. Bring this mixture to a boil and simmer uncovered for 15 minutes or until the mixture is as thick as jam. Cool. Take one half of the chilled dough and press it against the bottom and sides of a 9-inch cake pan. Spread cranberry mixture over the dough in the bottom of pan. Roll out remaining dough to ¼-inch thickness on a floured board. Cut it into strips and arrange them in a lattice pattern over the cranberry mixture. Decorate the top with the whole nuts. Bake tart in a pre-heated 375 °F oven for 40 minutes or until brown. Serve the tart with a dab of sour cream. Serves 6.

PEACH CRISP WITH HARD SAUCE
SOUTH

1 *lb. sliced peeled peaches*	4 *oz. brown sugar*
2 *teaspoons lemon juice*	2½ *oz. butter*
2 *oz. sifted flour*	*hard sauce (recipe below)*
2 *oz. rolled oats*	

Put peaches in a shallow baking dish; sprinkle with lemon juice. Mix flour, oats and brown sugar in a bowl. Cut in butter with a pastry blender. Press mixture over peaches; bake in a pre-heated 325 °F oven until peaches are tender, about 35 minutes. Serve warm with hard sauce. Serves 8.

Hard Sauce

2 *oz. butter*	1 *tablespoon brandy*
3 *oz. icing sugar*	

Rub butter with back of spoon in a mixing bowl until very creamy. Stir in the sugar very gradually. Heat brandy in a saucepan to just below a boil. Stir in butter mixture very gradually. Pile sauce on a dish, chill thoroughly.

GEORGIA PECAN PIE
SOUTH

3½ *oz. sugar*	1 *oz. butter*
1 *tablespoon cornflour*	3 *eggs, lightly beaten*
¼ *teaspoon salt*	8 *oz. whole pecan nuts*
14½ *oz. dark syrup*	1 *unbaked pie shell*

Mix sugar, cornflour and salt together in a mixing bowl. Add syrup, butter and eggs. Stir to mix. Scatter pecan nuts over the bottom of the pie shell. Beat filling with egg beater to blend thoroughly; pour mixture over nuts. Bake in a preheated 350 °F oven until set, about 1 hour.

PECAN PIE
ALL AMERICAN

1 *unbaked 9-inch pastry shell*
4 *oz. pecan halves*
3 *eggs beaten*
3½ *oz. sugar*
11 *oz. dark corn syrup*

¼ *teaspoon salt*
1 *teaspoon vanilla*
2 *oz. melted butter or margarine*

Prepare unbaked pastry shell. Spread nuts in bottom of pastry shell. Combine remaining ingredients and pour over nuts. Bake in a 375 °F oven 30 to 40 minutes or until filling appears set when the pie is gently moved. Makes one 9-inch pie. Serves 8.

PUMPKIN PIE
ALL AMERICAN

1 *unbaked 8-inch pastry shell*
½ *lb. canned pumpkin*
½ *teaspoon cinnamon*
¼ *teaspoon ginger*
¼ *teaspoon nutmeg*
⅛ *teaspoon cloves*

8 *fl. oz. milk or evaporated milk*
3½ *oz. sugar*
1 *egg, slightly beaten*
½ *teaspoon salt*

Prepare pastry shell. Blend pumpkin and spices thoroughly. Stir in remaining ingredients. Mix well. Pour into pastry shell. Bake at 400 °F about 1 hour. Pie is done when a table knife inserted in centre comes out clean. Filling may be soft but will set on cooling. Makes one 8-inch pie. Serves 6.

FRESH PERSIMMON PUDDING
MIDWEST

8 *oz. persimmon pulp*   2 *oz. walnuts*
7 *oz. sugar*   24 *crushed graham crackers*

Combine all the ingredients in a bowl. Allow to stand in the refrigerator for 12 hours before serving.

PINEAPPLE MENEHUNE
HAWAIIAN

4 *tablespoons brown sugar*   1 *very ripe pineapple*
4 *tablespoons flaked toasted*   3 *egg yolks*
   almonds   6 *oz. butter*
rum

Peel the pineapple and cut fruit into thin slices. Soak the slices for an hour or more in 4 fluid ounces of rum. Make a sauce by stirring the egg yolks with the butter in the top of a double boiler over simmering water. When the mixture is well blended, add the sugar and 4 tablespoons rum and continue to stir until the sauce begins to thicken and coat the spatula. Remove from heat. Drain the pineapple slices and arrange them on a long serving platter. Pour the sauce on the pineapple and sprinkle with almonds. Chill in the refrigerator before serving.

PUMPKIN PIE
MIDWEST

12 oz. canned pumpkin
6 oz. sugar
1 teaspoon cinnamon
½ teaspoon salt
½ teaspoon ground ginger
¼ teaspoon nutmeg

¼ teaspoon cloves
3 eggs, lightly beaten
½ pt milk
1 can (6 oz.) evaporated milk
1 9-inch unbaked pastry shell

Thoroughly mix pumpkin, sugar, spices and salt together in a bowl. Blend in egg, milk and evaporated milk. Pour into a pastry shell with high crimped edges. Bake in a pre-heated 400°F oven until knife comes out clean and custard is well set, about 50 minutes. Cool before serving.

RAISIN-NUT BREAD PUDDING
ALL AMERICAN

¾ pt milk
½ oz. butter or margarine
2 oz. brown sugar
1 teaspoon cinnamon
½ teaspoon nutmeg
½ teaspoon vanilla
2 egg yolks, slightly beaten

4 slices bread, cut in 1-inch cubes
2 oz. raisins
2 oz. slivered almonds
2 egg whites
¼ teaspoon salt

Heat milk; stir in fat, sugar, cinnamon, nutmeg and vanilla. Stir a little of the milk mixture into egg yolks. Then stir yolks into rest of milk mixture. Add bread cubes, raisins and half the nuts. Beat egg whites until foamy. Add salt and beat until stiff but not dry. Fold egg whites into pudding mixture. Pour into greased 1¼-pint casserole. Sprinkle top with rest of

nuts. Place casserole in pan of hot water. Bake at 325 °F 1¼ to
1½ hours, or until the tip of a knife inserted in the centre comes
out clean. Serves 6.

RHODE ISLAND JOHNNY CAKE
NEW ENGLAND

5 *oz. white cornmeal*	4 *fl. oz. milk*
1 *tablespoon salt*	8 *fl. oz. boiling water*

Stir meal and salt into water. Cook, stirring, until thick.
Remove from heat and stir in the milk. Drop in tablespoons
on to hot, greased, griddle. Brown lightly on each side and
serve with butter or syrup. 12 cakes.

RHUBARB SHERBET
FARWEST

½ *lb. rhubarb, coarsely cut*	2 *egg yolks, slightly beaten*
6 *oz. sugar*	1 *tablespoon lemon juice*
⅛ *teaspoon salt*	¼ *teaspoon vanilla*
8 *fl. oz. medium heavy cream*	2 *egg whites*

Combine unpeeled rhubarb, two-thirds of the sugar and the
salt in a pan. Cover it and simmer (without water) until
rhubarb is tender. Cool. Combine cream, egg yolks, lemon
juice and vanilla. Mix with rhubarb and pour into a pan.
Freeze this mixture until it is mushy in the freezer of the
refrigerator at coldest setting. Beat egg whites in a bowl,
gradually adding the remaining one-third of sugar; continue
beating until they are stiff. Turn the frozen mixture into a
chilled bowl, beat until smooth without melting. Fold in egg
whites and return mixture to freezer. Freeze until firm.
Serves 6.

SHOOFLY PIE
PENNSYLVANIA DUTCH

$3\frac{1}{2}$ *oz. sugar*
1 *oz. sifted plain flour*
$\frac{1}{8}$ *teaspoon salt*
$1\frac{1}{2}$ *oz. shortening*
1 *egg*

3 *tablespoons molasses*
2 *tablespoons boiling water*
$\frac{1}{2}$ *teaspoon baking soda*
1 *8-inch unbaked pie shell*

Mix the flour, sugar, salt and shortening together to form a coarse meal. Beat egg until light and fluffy. Add molasses, boiling water and soda and beat until soda is dissolved. Reserve half the crumb mixture. Add remainder to the molasses mixture and stir well until well blended. Pour into unbaked pie shell, sprinkle top with reserved crumbs and bake in 375°F oven for 35 minutes.

SNITZ KLOES
PENNSYLVANIA DUTCH

1 *lb. fresh pears*
6 *cloves*
2 *sticks cinnamon*
$1\frac{1}{2}$ *oz. fresh ginger root*
$3\frac{1}{2}$ *oz. sugar*
$1\frac{1}{2}$ *lb. grated bread*
$\frac{1}{2}$ *lb. chopped suet*

4 *oz. brown sugar*
2 *eggs*
$\frac{1}{4}$ *tablespoon flour*
$\frac{1}{2}$ *teaspoon cinnamon*
$\frac{1}{2}$ *teaspoon salt*
2 *teaspoons baking powder*

Pare fruit, core, and cook with spices and a little water until tender. Mix bread crumbs, suet, brown sugar and eggs and add flour sifted with cinnamon, salt and baking powder. Place pudding mixture in a basin, pour fruit over it, cover tightly and steam for 3 hours. Serves 8.

SWEET POTATO PIE
SOUTH

$3\frac{1}{2}$ oz. sugar
1 *teaspoon cinnamon*
$\frac{1}{2}$ *teaspoon allspice*
$\frac{1}{2}$ *teaspoon salt*
$\frac{1}{4}$ *teaspoon mace*
1 *lb. cooked sweet potatoes, mashed*

2 *eggs, lightly beaten*
8 *fl. oz. milk*
1 *oz. butter, melted*
1 *9-inch unbaked pastry shell*

Mix sugar, cinnamon, allspice, salt and mace. Add sweet potatoes. Combine eggs, milk and melted butter. Add to sweet potato mixture. Pour into pastry shell. Bake in 400 °F oven until filling is set, about 40 minutes.

SWEET POTATOES IN ORANGE SHELLS
ALL AMERICAN

3 *oranges*
1 *can* (1 *lb.*) *sweet potatoes, undrained*
1 *oz. butter or margarine, melted*

3 *tablespoons brown sugar, packed*
$\frac{1}{2}$ *teaspoon salt*
2 *tablespoons flaked coconut*
6 *miniature marshmallows*

Squeeze oranges; save juice. Remove membranes from orange shells. Mash sweet potatoes. Blend in 3 tablespoons orange juice, fat, brown sugar and salt. Stir into coconut. Spoon sweet potato mixture into the orange shells. Place in a shallow baking pan. Bake in a 350 °F oven for 20 to 30 minutes, or until lightly browned on top. Top with marshmallows and bake about 5 minutes longer to melt and brown marshmallows. Serves 6.

UPSIDE-DOWN CAKE
ALL AMERICAN

1 *oz. butter or margarine*
4 *oz. brown sugar*
6 *drained canned peach halves*
6 *drained maraschino cherries,*
  halved

12 *pecan halves*
quick coffee cake batter (see p.
  241)

Melt fat in a 9-inch layer cake pan over low heat. Sprinkle brown sugar over fat. Arrange fruit and nuts in sugar mixture. Prepare coffee cake batter and pour over fruit; spread evenly. Bake in a pre-heated 350 °F oven 30 to 40 minutes. Loosen cake from sides of pan and invert on serving plate. Allow to cool 5 minutes before removing pan. Serves 6.

VANILLA CREAM PIE
ALL AMERICAN

1 *8-inch pastry shell*
3 *level tablespoons cornflour*
2 *oz. sugar*
½ *teaspoon salt*
¾ *pt milk*

2 *egg yolks, beaten*
1 *oz. butter or margarine*
1 *teaspoon vanilla*
4 *fl. oz. whipping cream*
1 *tablespoon icing sugar*

Prepare, bake and cool pastry shell. Mix cornflour, sugar and salt in a heavy saucepan. Gradually stir in milk. Cook over moderate heat, stirring constantly, until thickened. Simmer 1 minute longer. Stir a little of the hot mixture into egg yolks; then stir yolks into remaining hot mixture. Cook 1 minute longer, stirring constantly. Stir in fat and vanilla. Set saucepan in cold water to cool. Stir frequently. Change water occasionally. Pour filling into pastry shell. Chill thoroughly. Before serving, whip cream until stiff and beat in icing sugar. Spread over pie. Makes one 8-inch pie. Serves 6.

VINEGAR PIE
MIDWEST

I *oz. butter*
3½ *oz. sugar*
3 *oz. flour*
½ *teaspoon ground cloves*
½ *teaspoon allspice*

I *egg*
2 *tablespoons vinegar*
8 *fl. oz. water*
I 8-*inch baked pastry shell*

Cream butter and sugar in a mixing bowl. Add flour, cloves, allspice, egg, vinegar and water to butter mixture, in that order. Pour into a double saucepan, cook until thick (about 15 minutes). Pour into a pastry shell (pre-baked about 3 minutes). Bake pie in a moderate, pre-heated 350 °F oven until set, about 30 minutes.

VERMONT STYLE INDIAN PUDDING
NEW ENGLAND

32 *fl. oz. milk*
4 *oz. dark molasses*
2½ *oz. yellow cornmeal*
2 *oz. sugar*

I *oz. butter*
¾ *teaspoon salt*
½ *teaspoon cinnamon, ground*
¼ *teaspoon nutmeg, ground*

Heat 24 fluid ounces of milk in the top of a double boiler. Add remaining ingredients. Cook over hot water, stirring occasionally, until mixture thickens, about 20 minutes. Pour into a casserole or oven dish, add remaining milk, without stirring. Bake in 300 °F oven for 2½ hours. Serve warm with cream, or with ice cream and maple syrup. Serves 6–8.

ZWETSCHENKUCHEN
PENNSYLVANIA DUTCH

8 *oz. sifted flour*
$\frac{1}{2}$ *teaspoon salt*
$\frac{1}{2}$ *teaspoon baking powder*
2 *teaspoons sugar*

5 *oz. butter*
2 *egg yolks*
$\frac{1}{2}$ *gill cold water*
bread crumbs

Filling

2 *lb. fresh purple plums*
5 *oz. sugar*
2 *egg yolks*

2 *tablespoons sugar*
2 *tablespoons cream*

Sift flour, salt and baking powder together. Cut in butter. Make well in centre, add egg yolks and water with palm of hand. Turn out on well-floured board and knead 5 minutes. Chill. Roll into thin sheet and cover bottom of cake pan. Sprinkle with bread crumbs and dot with butter. Cut plums in half, remove stones. Place in rows on bread crumbs in pan. Sprinkle with sugar and cover with mixture of egg yolks, sugar and cream beaten together. Bake at 350°F for 50 minutes.

Cakes

ANGEL FOOD CAKE
MIDWEST

4 oz. sifted flour
5 oz. sifted icing sugar
6 egg whites
1½ teaspoons cream of tartar

¼ teaspoon salt
1½ teaspoons vanilla
¼ teaspoon almond extract
5 oz. granulated sugar

Pre-heat oven to 375°F. Sift flour and icing sugar together four times. Beat egg whites, cream of tartar, salt, vanilla, and almond extract until the egg whites form soft peaks. Beat in the granulated sugar 2 tablespoons at a time. Beat mixture until egg whites are stiff and glossy. Fold in flour-sugar mixture carefully. Spoon batter into clean, dry, 9-inch tube pan. Bake 30 minutes. Invert pan, cool 1 hour and then remove cake from pan.

APPLESAUCE CAKE
FARWEST

4 oz. shortening
7 oz. sugar
1 egg, well beaten
7 oz. plain flour
1 teaspoon baking soda
1 teaspoon cinnamon
½ teaspoon salt

½ teaspoon ground cloves
5 oz. chopped walnuts or 5 oz.
  chopped filberts
4 oz. raisins
8 fl. oz. thickened unsweetened
  apple sauce

Cream shortening in a large bowl. Add sugar to shortening and cream until well blended. Add the egg to mixture; mix well. Sift flour, soda, salt and spices together on a piece of waxed paper. Add gradually to the egg mixture, stirring after each addition. Add the remaining ingredients and beat batter thoroughly. Pour into a greased baking tin (8 inch by 8 inch by 2 inch). Bake in a moderate oven (350°F) for 1 hour or until done. Serves 8.

CHOCOLATE CAKE
ALL AMERICAN

7 oz. cake flour
9 oz. sugar
1 teaspoon salt
1 teaspoon baking soda
4 oz. softened butter or margarine

8 fl. oz. milk
1 teaspoon vanilla
2 eggs
2 or 3 oz. (2 or 3 squares) unsweetened chocolate, melted

Mix dry ingredients well. Add fat and half of the milk; beat until creamy. Mix in remaining milk, vanilla and eggs. Add chocolate; beat until creamy. Pour into two 8-inch greased and floured layer-cake pans. Bake at 350°F in a pre-heated oven 30 to 35 minutes, or until cake surface springs back when touched lightly. Cool cake a few minutes before removing from pans. When cool, frost with creamy chocolate frosting. Makes two 8-inch layers.

Note: For a loaf cake, use a greased and floured 9 by 12 inch cake pan. Bake about 40 minutes.

Creamy Frosting
White

10 oz. icing sugar
2½ oz. softened butter or margarine

3 tablespoons milk
1 teaspoon vanilla

Beat about 8 ounces of sugar with all other ingredients in a mixing bowl until frosting is creamy and smooth. Beat in enough of the remaining sugar for a frosting that will spread evenly. Spread on cooled cake.

Chocolate Frosting – Mix in 1 or 2 ounces (1 or 2 squares) of melted chocolate. Or increase milk to 2 fluid ounces and use $1\frac{1}{2}$ ounces cocoa. Beat until creamy and smooth.

QUICK COFFEE CAKE
ALL AMERICAN

$1\frac{1}{2}$ oz. softened butter or margarine	$\frac{1}{4}$ teaspoon salt
	$\frac{1}{2}$ gill milk
$3\frac{1}{2}$ oz. granulated sugar	$\frac{1}{4}$ teaspoon vanilla
1 egg	$2\frac{1}{2}$ oz. brown sugar
4 oz. flour	$\frac{1}{2}$ teaspoon cinnamon
$1\frac{1}{4}$ teaspoons baking powder	1 oz. butter or margarine

Mix fat with granulated sugar. Add egg and beat until creamy. Mix flour, baking powder and salt thoroughly; add to sugar mixture alternately with milk. Add vanilla. Spread batter evenly in a greased 8-inch square baking pan. Mix brown sugar and cinnamon and sprinkle over batter. Dot with 1 ounce fat. Bake in a pre-heated 350°F oven for 25 to 30 minutes. Makes 6 servings.

DEVIL'S FOOD CAKE
ALL AMERICAN

9 oz. sifted cake flour	3 eggs
3 tablespoons cocoa	1 tablespoon baking soda
$\frac{1}{2}$ teaspoon salt	4 fl. oz. milk
14 oz. sugar	8 fl. oz. boiling water
4 oz. shortening	

Pre-heat oven to 350°F. Grease and flour the bottom of a 12 inch by 9 inch baking pan. Sift together flour, cocoa and salt. Add sugar to shortening: cream well. Add eggs one at a time, creaming after each addition. Combine baking soda and milk. Add alternately with flour mixture to creamed mixture, beating after each addition. Pour into prepared pan. Bake for 40 minutes. Cool on wire rack. Ice with chocolate frosting.

GINGERBREAD
NEW ENGLAND

4 *oz. shortening*	$\frac{1}{2}$ *teaspoon salt*
4 *oz. brown sugar*	$\frac{3}{4}$ *teaspoon baking soda*
1 *egg*	$\frac{1}{2}$ *teaspoon ginger*
6 *oz. light molasses*	$\frac{1}{2}$ *teaspoon cinnamon*
6 *oz. flour*	4 *fl. oz. boiling water*

Beat shortening and sugar until creamy. Add egg and molasses; beat well. Mix dry ingredients thoroughly. Add to molasses mixture alternately with boiling water. Beat after each addition. Pour batter into a greased 8 by 8 by 2 inch baking pan. Bake in a pre-heated 350°F oven 35 to 40 minutes. Serve warm. Serves 6 to 9.

JAM CAKE
SOUTH

1 *lb. flour*	14 *oz. sugar*
1 *teaspoon ground cloves*	4 *eggs*
1 *teaspoon allspice*	8 *fl. oz. buttermilk*
1 *teaspoon grated nutmeg*	1 *teaspoon baking soda*
$\frac{1}{4}$ *teaspoon salt*	8 *oz. blackberry jam*
8 *oz. shortening*	8 *oz. broken nuts*

Sift flour, cloves, allspice, nutmeg and salt together on to waxed paper. Cream shortening and sugar together in a mixing bowl. Add eggs; beat until light and fluffy. Mix soda with buttermilk in a cup. Add flour and buttermilk mixtures alternately to shortening, sugar and egg mixture starting and ending with flour mixture. Fold in jam and nuts. Pour into a greased and floured 10-inch tube pan. Bake in a pre-heated 350°F oven for 1 hour.

NUT BREAD
ALL AMERICAN

5 oz. sugar	½ teaspoon salt
2 oz. shortening	8 fl. oz. orange juice or milk
2 eggs	½ teaspoon vanilla
8 oz. flour	3 oz. chopped nuts
3 teaspooons baking powder	

Beat sugar, shortening and eggs together in a bowl until creamy. Mix flour, baking powder and salt thoroughly. Stir into egg mixture alternately with liquid and vanilla; stir nuts into last portion of flour mixture before blending it into batter. Pour into a greased 9 by 5 by 3 inch loaf pan. Bake at 350°F in a pre-heated oven 50 to 60 minutes, or until no batter clings to needle inserted in centre of loaf. Remove from pan and cool on rack. Makes 1 loaf.

SALLY LUNN
MID-ATLANTIC

2 fl. oz. warm water	3 tablespoons white sugar
½ oz. yeast	1 teaspoon salt
3 eggs	3 oz. flour
¾ pt milk	4 oz. melted butter

Dissolve yeast in 2 fluid ounces warm water. Separate eggs and beat yolks and whites separately until the yolks have become light yellow and the whites have begun to stiffen. Mix together. Cream yeast, add to egg mixture with milk, sugar, salt. Beat in flour until stiff batter is made. Add melted butter, beat again. Cover, place in warm place until dough has doubled. Beat batter again. Pour into large greased funnel pan or muffin tins. Allow to rise until dough has nearly doubled again. Bake in 400 °F oven until a knife run into the cake comes out clean, about 30 minutes. Serve hot to be cut at table. Makes 1 large cake.

SPICED PRUNE CAKE
ALL AMERICAN

1 *package spice cake mix (for 2-layer cake)* 5 *oz. drained, pitted and chopped prunes*

Prepare the cake batter according to package directions. Thoroughly mix prunes into cake batter. Pour batter into two greased and floured 8- or 9-inch layer-cake pans. Bake according to package directions but increase baking time by 10 minutes. Cool cake a few minutes before removing from the pans. When cool frost with creamy white frosting. Makes two 8- or 9-inch layers.

STRAWBERRY SHORTCAKE
MID-ATLANTIC

1 *lb. strawberries* 3 *oz. shortening*
2 *oz. finely granulated sugar* 4 *oz. butter*
8 *oz. sifted flour* 2½ *fl. oz. milk*
3 *teaspoons baking powder* 2 *tablespoons sugar*
1 *teaspoon salt* 1 *pt whipped cream*

Cakes

Wash and hull strawberries. Slice in half lengthwise, put in a bowl and sprinkle with finely granulated sugar. Sift flour, baking powder, salt and remaining sugar together. Cut in shortening and add milk. Mix lightly. Divide dough into two parts. Roll each ½ inch thick. Spread one part with 2 ounces butter and cover with other half. Bake in a small pan in a pre-heated 425°F oven until dough has risen and become golden (about 15 minutes). Separate layers and spread each with remaining butter and sweetened berries. Place layers together and cover with whipped cream and remaining berries. Serve at once. Serves 8.

VELVETY WHITE CAKE
ALL AMERICAN

8 oz. cake flour
9 oz. sugar
1 tablespoon baking powder
1 teaspoon salt
4 oz. softened butter or margarine or shortening

8 fl. oz. milk
4 egg whites, unbeaten
1 teaspoon vanilla
¼ teaspoon almond extract, if desired

Mix dry ingredients well. Add fat and half of the milk; beat until creamy. Add remaining milk, egg whites and flavouring; beat until creamy. Pour into two 8-inch greased and floured layer-cake pans. Bake in a pre-heated 375°F oven 25 to 30 minutes, or until the cake surface springs back when touched lightly. Cool cake for a few minutes before removing from the pans. When cool, frost as desired. Makes two 8-inch layers.

CARAMEL NUT FROSTING
ALL AMERICAN

4 *oz. butter or margarine*
7 *oz. brown sugar*
2 *fl. oz. milk*
9 *oz. icing sugar*

3 *oz. finely chopped pecans or*
  walnuts
½ *teaspoon vanilla*
nut halves, as desired

Combine fat, brown sugar and milk in a saucepan. Cook over medium heat, stirring constantly, only until mixture boils and sugar is dissolved. Cool slightly. Beat icing sugar into cooked mixture until frosting reaches spreading consistency. Add chopped nuts and vanilla; mix well. Spread on cooled cake. Garnish with nut halves. For 8-inch layer cake or 9 by 12 inch loaf cake.

Cookies
(Biscuits)

BROWNIES
MID-WEST

4 *oz. butter*	1 *teaspoon vanilla extract*
2 *oz. unsweetened chocolate*	3 *oz. sifted plain flour*
2 *eggs*	$\frac{1}{2}$ *teaspoon baking powder*
7 *oz. sugar*	$\frac{1}{4}$ *teaspoon salt*

Melt butter and chocolate together over hot water; cool. Beat eggs and sugar together in a bowl until light and fluffy. Beat in chocolate mixture and vanilla. Sift together flour, baking powder and salt on to a piece of waxed paper. Stir flour mixture into chocolate mixture. Spread mixture evenly in a lightly greased 8-inch square pan. Bake in a pre-heated 350°F oven for 30 minutes. Cool 1 minute and cut into squares with a sharp knife. Makes 16 brownies. May be iced with chocolate icing if desired.

CHOCOLATE SPARKLES
ALL AMERICAN

8 *oz. softened butter or mar-garine*	$\frac{1}{2}$ *teaspoon vanilla*
	11 *oz. flour*
$8\frac{1}{2}$ *oz. sugar*	2 *teaspoons cream of tartar*
2 *eggs*	1 *teaspoon baking soda*
2 *oz. (2 squares) unsweetened chocolate, melted*	$\frac{1}{2}$ *teaspoon salt*
	$1\frac{1}{2}$ *oz. sugar*

247

Beat fat and 8½ ounces sugar until creamy. Beat in eggs; add melted chocolate and vanilla. Mix flour, cream of tartar, soda and salt. Stir into chocolate mixture. Blend well. Chill dough. Shape dough into balls about 1 inch in diameter. Roll balls in 1½ ounces sugar and place about 2 inches apart on an ungreased baking sheet. Bake in a pre-heated 400°F oven 8 to 10 minutes. Remove from baking sheet while warm. Makes 5 or 6 dozen cookies.

Cinnamon-sugar Cookies – Omit chocolate. Roll balls of dough in a mixture of 1½ ounces sugar and 1 tablespoon cinnamon; bake as directed.

Chocolate Chip Cookies – In place of 10 ounces granulated sugar, use 3½ ounces granulated sugar and 7 ounces brown sugar. Beat sugars with butter or margarine. Omit chocolate. Stir 3 ounces chopped nuts and 12 ounces chocolate chips into the dough. Drop dough from a teaspoon on to an ungreased baking sheet and bake as directed.

MOLASSES SNAPS
ALL AMERICAN

6 *oz. shortening*	½ *teaspoon salt*
8 *oz. brown sugar*	½ *teaspoon cloves*
2 *eggs*	1 *teaspoon cinnamon*
3 *oz. light molasses*	1 *teaspoon ginger*
9 *oz. flour*	2 *oz. chopped nuts, if desired*
2 *teaspoons baking soda*	2 *oz. raisins, if desired*

Beat shortening and sugar until creamy. Beat in eggs and molasses. Mix dry ingredients and stir in raisins and nuts, if used. Stir flour mixture into molasses mixture. Drop dough from a teaspoon on to a lightly greased baking sheet; space cookies about 2 inches apart. Bake in a pre-heated 375 °F oven 10 to 12 minutes or until set but not hard. Remove from baking sheet while warm. Makes 3 to 4 dozen cookies.

BLUEBERRY MUFFINS
MID-ATLANTIC

1 *lb. blueberries*	$\frac{1}{2}$ *teaspoon salt*
8 *oz. flour*	1 *egg*
3 *tablespoons sugar*	6 *fl. oz. milk*
3 *tablespoons baking powder*	1$\frac{1}{2}$ *oz. melted shortening*

Wash the berries and drain thoroughly. Sift flour, sugar, baking powder and salt together. Beat egg and add milk and stir into dry ingredients. Do not beat, should be lumpy. Add melted shortening and blueberries. Grease about 25 muffin tins and fill two-thirds full. Bake in a 350 °F oven until high and brown, about 20 minutes. Serve with butter.

MUFFINS
ALL AMERICAN

1 *egg*	1 *tablespoon baking powder*
8 *fl. oz. milk*	1 *teaspoon salt*
2$\frac{1}{2}$ *oz. oil or shortening melted*	2 *oz. sugar*
8 *oz. flour*	

Beat egg until yolk and white are well blended. Blend in milk and fat. Mix dry ingredients thoroughly. Add liquid and stir until dry ingredients are barely moistened. Do not overmix. Batter should be lumpy. Fill greased muffin tins half-full of batter. Bake at 400 °F oven 20 to 25 minutes. Makes 12 muffins.

Bran Muffins – Reduce flour to 5 ounces. Mix 6 ounces bran flakes or raisin bran cereal with dry ingredients before adding liquid.

Oatmeal-Raisin Muffins – Reduce flour to 5 ounces. Mix 3 ounces quick-cooking oats and 2 ounces raisins with dry ingredients before adding liquid.

OATMEAL COOKIES
ALL AMERICAN

4 oz. flour	7 oz. brown sugar
1¼ teaspoons baking powder	1 egg
½ teaspoon baking soda	¾ teaspoon vanilla
½ teaspoon salt	4½ oz. quick-cooking oats
4 oz. shortening	

Mix flour, baking powder, soda and salt. Beat shortening and sugar until creamy. Beat in egg and vanilla. Blend in flour mixture. Stir in rolled oats. Chill. Shape dough into balls about 1 inch in diameter. Place about 2 inches apart on an ungreased cookie sheet. Bake in a pre-heated 350°F oven for 10 to 15 minutes. Remove from baking sheet while still warm. Makes 3 to 4 dozen cookies.

Cookies (Biscuits)

OREILLE DE COCHON
CREOLE

4 oz. plain flour
¼ teaspoon salt
2 fl. oz. water

deep fat for frying
½ pt. pure cane syrup (see method)

Sift flour and salt together in a bowl. Add sufficient water (about 2 fluid ounces) to make a stiff dough. Cut off a small portion of dough about the size of a walnut. Roll out dough very, very thin on a floured board. Twist the centre of each piece of rolled-out dough, so that it resembles a pig's ear. Drop each into 375 °F fat and fry until very light brown (about 3 minutes). Boil the syrup in a heavy pan until soft-ball stage (alternatively use 10 ounces white sugar and ½ pint water and boil this mixture until soft-ball stage). Dip each 'ear' in the hot syrup and place it on a rack to cool.

PEANUT BUTTER COOKIES
ALL AMERICAN

8 oz. shortening
8 oz. peanut butter
7 oz. granulated sugar
7 oz. brown sugar
2 eggs

1 teaspoon vanilla
9½ oz. flour
¾ teaspoon baking soda
½ teaspoon baking powder

Beat shortening and peanut butter in a mixing bowl until creamy. Gradually add sugars, beating thoroughly after each addition. Beat in eggs and vanilla. Mix remaining ingredients and blend into peanut butter mixture. Shape dough into balls about 1 inch diameter. Place about 2 inches apart on an ungreased baking sheet. Flatten each cookie. Criss-cross top of each cookie with a fork, if desired. Bake in a pre-heated 375 °F oven 10 to 15 minutes. Remove from baking sheet while warm. Makes 4 to 5 dozen cookies.

Recipes

PRETZELS
MIDWEST

8 *oz. butter*
10 *oz. sifted flour*
6 *eggs, well beaten*
½ *gill cream*
1 *teaspoon vanilla*

7 *oz. sugar*
½ *teaspoon salt*
1 *egg white for icing*
1 *tablespoon milk for icing*

Cut shortening into flour in a mixing bowl, as though making a pie crust. Combine eggs, cream and vanilla. Mix in sugar and salt. Add to flour and shortening mixture; chill. Form the dough into rolls 8 inches long and about as thick as a pencil. Shape into pretzel form (an open symmetrical knot). Mix egg white and milk together in a dish. Brush the pretzels with this mixture. Bake in a 350°F oven until brown, about 14 minutes. Makes about 5 dozen pretzels.

BAKING POWDER BISCUITS
ALL AMERICAN

8 *oz. flour*
1 *tablespoon baking powder*
1 *teaspoon salt*

2½ *oz. shortening*
6 *fl. oz. milk*

Mix dry ingredients thoroughly. Mix in fat only until mixture is crumbly. Add most of the milk and stir to mix. Add more milk as needed to make a dough that is soft but too sticky to knead. Knead dough gently on a lightly floured surface 10 to 12 times. Form into a ball. Pat or roll dough to ½ to ¾ inch thickness. Cut with a floured biscuit cutter or cut into squares with a knife. Place on an ungreased baking sheet about 1 inch apart for crusty biscuits; together for softer biscuits. Bake in a pre-heated 450°F oven 12 to 15 minutes, or until golden brown. Makes 12 biscuits.

Note: These are very similar to English scones.

Cookies (Biscuits)

BUTTERMILK BISCUITS
MOUNTAIN

8 oz. flour
2 teaspoons baking powder
1 teaspoon salt
½ teaspoon baking soda

4 oz. shortening
1 gill buttermilk
1 tablespoon melted bacon fat

Sift flour, baking powder, salt and soda together in a mixing bowl. Cut in shortening, until mixture resembles coarse crumbs. Add buttermilk immediately; stir until dough just stiffens. Pat out ½ inch thick on lightly floured board and cut with biscuit cutter. Place biscuits on a greased baking sheet; brush tops with bacon fat. Bake in a pre-heated 450°F oven until high and brown, about 15 minutes. Makes about 18 biscuits.

BEATEN BISCUITS
SOUTH

1 lb. flour
½ teaspoon salt

8 oz. chilled lard
4 fl. oz. iced water

Sift flour with salt then quickly cut lard into mixture with two knives or pastry blender. Mix in enough water to make a very stiff dough. Lightly flour a board and beat the biscuits with a rolling pin, pestle or wooden mallet. As the dough is beaten thin, fold it, and continue beating until it is very elastic, about 300 hard strokes (more strokes make a lighter biscuit). Roll the dough ½ inch thick and cut biscuits about 1¼ inch in diameter. Prick each biscuit with a kitchen fork. Bake in a 350°F oven until a light brown, about 20 minutes. Makes about 30 biscuits.

Breads, Batters etc.

BUCKWHEAT CAKES
MOUNTAIN

$\frac{1}{2}$ oz. yeast
1$\frac{1}{2}$ pts lukewarm water
10 oz. buckwheat flour
2 oz. wheat flour

2 teaspoons sugar
1 teaspoon baking soda
4 fl. oz. milk
4 fl. oz. warm water

Combine yeast and the 1$\frac{1}{2}$ pints of lukewarm water in a mixing bowl. Thicken to a stiff batter with the flours. Cover and let it rise overnight. Next day, dissolve sugar and soda in the milk. Add to the batter and moisten with enough warm water to make a thin batter. Pour on a medium-hot greased griddle to form a 6-inch cake. Turn once when browned.

Renew batter at night by reserving at least 8 fluid ounces as a starter. Add 8 fluid ounces lukewarm water, 3 ounces buckwheat flour, and 1 ounce wheat flour. The next day proceed with soda, sugar, milk and water as above. Every three or four days add a $\frac{1}{4}$ teaspoon of yeast to keep the batter going.

CALAS
CREOLE

1$\frac{1}{4}$ pts water
4 oz. raw rice
$\frac{1}{2}$ oz. compressed yeast
4 fl. oz. warm water
3 eggs, well beaten
2$\frac{1}{2}$ oz. granulated sugar

1 oz. sifted flour
1 teaspoon salt
$\frac{1}{4}$ teaspoon nutmeg
1 oz. icing sugar
fat for deep frying

Bring the $1\frac{1}{4}$ pints of water to boiling. Add rice to the boiling water and cook until the rice is very soft (about 1 hour). Allow to cool, then pass it through a food mill. Combine the rice with the yeast in the warm water. Cover the bowl and allow the mixture to rise for 12 hours. Add eggs, flour, granulated sugar, salt and nutmeg to rice. Beat mixture thoroughly. Cover bowl with a cloth and allow to rise in a warm place for 25 minutes. Drop by tablespoons into 360 °F fat and fry until brown (about 3 minutes). Drain and sprinkle with icing sugar. Makes 50 calas.

CORN BREAD
SOUTH

4 oz. sifted flour	1 egg
5 oz. yellow cornmeal	3 tablespoons sugar
2 teaspoons baking powder	8 fl. oz. sour milk or buttermilk
$\frac{1}{2}$ teaspoon baking soda	2 oz. melted shortening
$\frac{1}{2}$ teaspoon salt	

Sift flour, cornmeal, baking powder, soda and salt together in a mixing bowl. Cream egg with sugar in another bowl. Add buttermilk and shortening to egg-sugar mixture. Slowly combine with dry ingredients. Stir until ingredients are mixed but do not beat; work quickly. Grease a 9 by 9 by 2 inch pan well, dust with cornmeal. Pour cornmeal batter in pan; bake in a pre-heated hot oven (425 °F) until browned, about 25 minutes.

CORN BREAD
ALL AMERICAN

5 oz. yellow cornmeal	$\frac{1}{2}$ teaspoon salt
4 oz. flour	8 fl. oz. milk
4 teaspoons baking powder	1 egg, beaten
2 oz. sugar	2 oz. melted shortening or oil

Mix dry ingredients thoroughly. Combine milk and egg; stir in fat. Add liquid to dry ingredients; stir only enough to mix. Pour batter into a greased 8 by 8 by 2 inch baking tin. Bake in a pre-heated 400°F oven about 25 minutes or until lightly browned. Serves 6.

CORN PONE
MOUNTAIN

12½ oz. yellow cornmeal	¼ teaspoon baking soda
½ pt boiling water	2 eggs, well beaten
6 oz. molasses	5 oz. flour
4 oz. bacon drippings	2 teaspoons baking powder
8 oz. buttermilk	1 teaspoon salt
4 oz. cold water	

Place cornmeal in a bowl and pour boiling water over it. Add molasses and drippings; cool. In a bowl, combine milk, cold water and baking soda. Stir into the cornmeal. Add eggs, flour, baking powder, and salt. Beat mixture thoroughly. Pour into a large well-greased hot baking pan. Bake in a 375°F oven until brown and high, about 25 minutes. Cut into squares and serve hot.

CHEESE DROPS
MIDWEST

1 oz. butter	2 tablespoons grated cheese
¾ oz. flour	3 egg whites, beaten stiff
¼ teaspoon salt	paprika
3 drops red pepper sauce	

Melt the butter in a saucepan; add the flour and make a very light roux. Remove pan from the heat. Add seasonings and cheese, blending well. Fold in egg whites. Drop mixture from a tablespoon on to a greased sheet. Sprinkle drops liberally with paprika; bake in a pre-heated 360 °F oven until brown and set, about 10 minutes. Makes 2 dozen cheese drops.

CHEESE FRITTERS
MIDWEST

4 oz. flour	½ teaspoon salt
1½ teaspoons baking powder	4 slices processed cheese (about
1 egg, slightly beaten	¼ inch thick)
4 oz. milk	deep fat for frying

Sift flour and baking powder on to waxed paper. Mix egg, milk and salt together in a bowl. Add the flour and baking powder mixture. Dip cheese into the batter and fry in deep fat, 350 °F, until brown and puffed, about 3 minutes.

CRACKLING CORN BREAD I
MOUNTAIN

1¼ pts water	¼ teaspoon salt
8 oz. white cornmeal	8 oz. fat
4 oz. cracklings (the bits of meat that remain after lard has been rendered down)	

Bring water to boil in pan; slowly add cornmeal, stirring until thick. Add cracklings and seasonings. Cool until batter can be handled. Form into sticks, about the dimension of half a banana; fry in fat until brown. Crisp in a 400 °F oven.

CRACKLING CORN BREAD II
MOUNTAIN

½ lb. cracklings (meat which remains after fat is rendered from pork)*
8 oz. cornmeal
3 tablespoons flour

1 teaspoon salt
1 teaspoon baking soda
¾ pt buttermilk
1 egg, beaten

Mix cracklings with dry ingredients in a mixing bowl. Add buttermilk and egg. Beat until combined and pour into a hot greased ovenproof dish or baking tin. Bake in a pre-heated 450°F oven until light brown, about 25 minutes.
* If cracklings are unavailable, fried bacon, broken into pieces, may be substituted.

CUSH-CUSH WITH SUCRE BRULÉ
CREOLE

4 tablespoons cooking oil
10 oz. cornmeal
12 fl. oz. milk

1½ teaspoons salt
1 teaspoon baking powder
Sucre Brulé (recipe below)

Heat oil in a heavy iron pan. Mix other ingredients together in a bowl. Add to the oil and allow crust to form on the bottom of the pan. Stir mixture well, lower flame to simmer; cook for 15 minutes. Serve with Sucre Brulé or with cane syrup and a glass of cold milk for breakfast.

Sucre Brulé

7 oz. white sugar
8 fl. oz. water

2 fl. oz. boiled milk

Cook sugar until caramel stage. Carefully add water and boil mixture to a thin syrup. Add the boiled milk and serve hot over Cush-Cush.

DRECHTER KUCHA
PENNSYLVANIA DUTCH

2 eggs
¾ pt milk
¼ teaspoon salt

½ teaspoon baking powder
¾ lb. sifted plain flour

Beat egg and milk together with salt. Sift baking powder with flour, add liquid mixture gradually. Stir well to make smooth batter. Pour batter into funnel (keeping end closed). Allow batter to flow from funnel into hot fat (1 inch deep in pan). Start at centre and form helix the size of the pan, being careful not to let batter overlap and form solid cake. When cake rises, turn over and fry on other side. Serve hot with jelly.* Makes 2 dozen cakes.

* Jelly in this context would not be a gelatine-based jelly, but a jellied conserve.

GRITS
MOUNTAIN

8 oz. grits
1¼ pts water
1 teaspoon salt

2 fl. oz. milk
8 oz. butter

Put grits in a pan and cover with water. Soak overnight. Drain. Put the grits in a double boiler with 1¼ pints of water and salt. As the grits thicken, more water may be necessary to keep them from sticking. After an hour, add milk and continue to cook slowly for 30 minutes. Butter lavishly. Serves 4 for breakfast.

Recipes

HUSH PUPPIES
MOUNTAIN

8 oz. white cornmeal
4 oz. plain flour
1 tablespoon baking powder
1 teaspoon salt
¼ teaspoon pepper

2 medium eggs, beaten
6 oz. milk
1½ oz. chopped grated onion
2 oz. melted fat
fat for deep frying

Sift the dry ingredients together on a piece of waxed paper. Combine the eggs, milk, onion and 2 ounces fat in a mixing bowl. Add the dry ingredients and stir to blend, but don't beat. Make into 24 to 30 small balls, about 1½ tablespoons each. Fry in deep 350°F fat until brown, about 3 minutes. Drain on absorbent paper.

POOR BOY SANDWICH
CREOLE

1 hard crusted roll or section of French bread (about 6 inches)
1 clove garlic
1 teaspoon French mustard
6 slices lean cooked beef
6 slices Cheddar cheese

3 slices tomato, about ¼ inch thick
1 tablespoon shredded lettuce
1 tablespoon grated onion
1 teaspoon oil and vinegar salad dressing

Split roll or bread lengthwise. Rub garlic on inside. Spread each half with mustard. Layer meat, cheese, tomato, lettuce and onion on one half of roll or bread. Sprinkle it with dressing. Top with remaining half roll. Makes 1 sandwich.

MOLASSES WHEAT BREAD
WEST

8 *fl. oz. milk*	8 *fl. oz. warm water*
2 *tablespoons molasses*	12 *oz. whole wheat flour*
1 *tablespoon salt*	10 *oz. sifted plain flour*
1 *oz. dry yeast*	1½ *oz. soft shortening*

Scald milk. Pour into a large bowl with molasses and salt. Cool to lukewarm. Add yeast to warm water. Let stand 5 minutes. Add to milk mixture. Blend in all the whole wheat flour and 4 ounces of white flour with shortening. Beat 100 strokes. Slowly work in more flour, a little at a time until dough cleans bowl. Turn on to lightly floured cloth-covered board; knead until smooth. Place in a greased bowl. Turn to grease all sides of dough. Cover and let rise until double in size in a warm draught-free place, about 1 hour and 15 minutes. Knead lightly. Divide in two and shape like loaves. Place in two greased loaf pans 8½ by 4½ inches. Cover, let rise in warm place until centre of dough is slightly above pan edges, and dent remains when dough is gently pressed. Bake in a pre-heated 375 °F oven until well browned on all sides, about 40 minutes. Makes 2 loaves.

SPOON BREAD
MID-ATLANTIC

¾ *pt milk*	1 *teaspoon salt*
5 *oz. white cornmeal*	1 *teaspoon baking powder*
8 *fl. oz. milk*	3 *beaten egg yolks*
1 *oz. melted shortening*	3 *egg whites, beaten stiff*

Cook ¾ pint milk and corn meal together for about 35 minutes until very thick, stir constantly. Remove from heat and add remaining milk, shortening, salt and baking powder. Add egg yolks and then fold in whites. Bake in greased baking dish in a 325 °F oven until high and brown, about 1 hour. Serves 8. Spooned on plate, eaten buttered, with a fork.

PANCAKES
MIDWEST

8 *oz. flour*
4 *teaspoons baking powder*
1 *teaspoon salt*
2 *tablespoons sugar*

1 *egg, well beaten*
$\frac{3}{4}$ *pt milk*
$2\frac{1}{2}$ *oz. oil or melted fat*

Heat griddle while mixing batter. When griddle is hot enough, drops of water sprinkled on it will bounce. Mix dry ingredients thoroughly. Combine egg with milk and fat. Add to dry ingredients and stir only until combined. Batter will be lumpy. For each pancake, pour about 2 fluid ounces batter on to hot griddle. Cook until edges become slightly dry and bubbles form on top. Turn and brown the other side. Makes about 12 pancakes, $4\frac{1}{2}$ inches in diameter.

POPOVERS
NEW ENGLAND

2 *eggs*
4 *oz. plain flour*
pinch salt

8 *fl. oz. milk*
2 *teaspoons bacon fat*

Beat egg yolks and egg whites separately until yolks lighten and whites begin to stiffen. Sift flour and salt together twice. Gradually add milk, mixing well. Add eggs and fat, beat hard for 2 minutes. Pour mixture into 8 pre-heated, greased custard cups. Bake in very hot oven (450 °F) until popovers puff, about

15 minutes. Reduce heat to 350 °F and bake until brown, about
20 minutes. Serve as breakfast bread.

SOURDOUGH
WEST

Sponge or Starter

8 *oz. cornmeal*
$\frac{3}{4}$ *pt warm water*

$\frac{1}{2}$ *oz. dry yeast or equivalent*

Mix flour, water and yeast well. Place in warm dark place for
48 hours. Before using, remove $\frac{1}{2}$ cup of mixture and store in
a scalded, tightly covered jar in the refrigerator to start next
batch when required.

SOURDOUGH HOTCAKES

Starter as above (less $\frac{1}{2}$ cup)
8 *oz. flour*
$\frac{3}{4}$ *pt water*
1 *egg*

1 *teaspoon salt*
1 *teaspoon baking soda*
1 *tablespoon sugar*
2 *tablespoons melted lard*

The night before, add starter to flour and water. The following
day add egg, salt and sugar and beat together. Add fat and
baking soda. Bake on hot, lightly greased griddle. Turn once.
Serve with molasses. Serves 3.

SOURDOUGH BREAD

$\frac{1}{2}$ *cup starter (see above)*
1$\frac{1}{2}$ *lb. flour*
$\frac{3}{4}$ *pt warm water*
2 *tablespoons bacon fat*

2 *tablespoons sugar*
1 *teaspoon salt*
$\frac{1}{4}$ *teaspoon baking soda*
1 *tablespoon warm water*

Combine starter with $\frac{1}{2}$ pound of flour and $\frac{3}{4}$ pint of warm
water in a bowl. Allow to develop overnight. Combine fat with
sponge. Sift 1 pound of flour, sugar and salt together. Put in
mixing bowl; make well in centre. Pour sponge-fat mixture

into well. Combine with flour to make a soft dough. Knead on floured board for 15 minutes. Cover with a towel and let rise in a warm place until doubled, about 3 hours. Dissolve the soda and water; add to dough. Knead it thoroughly. Shape dough into loaves in bread pans and set aside to rise again. When doubled, bake at 375 °F until high and well browned, about 50 minutes.

SQUAW BREAD
SOUTHWEST

12 oz. flour	1 heaped tablespoon shortening
3 heaped teaspoons baking powder	¾ pt luke-warm water
1 teaspoon salt	deep fat for frying

Sift flour, baking powder and salt together in a mixing bowl. Cut in shortening, adding water to make dough. Do not over-mix. Roll out dough ½ inch thick; cut into 3-inch squares. Cut hole in the centre of each. Fry in 350 °F deep fat until high and brown, about 3 minutes.

TORTILLAS, TACOS, ENCHILADAS
SOUTHWEST

Tortillas

5 oz. cornmeal, masa or mixtamal	8 fl. oz. boiling water
	1 teaspoon salt

Add salt to water; add cornmeal. Bring quickly to a boil. Pat into rounds and cook on a lightly greased griddle or in a heavy iron frying pan, turning once.

Tacos

tortillas	oil for deep frying

Deep fry the tortillas in 350 °F fat until edges curl, about three minutes.

Enchiladas

6 *tortillas*	*fat for deep frying*
3 *tablespoons bacon fat*	4 *fl. oz. chilli sauce*
4 *oz. ground cooked meat*	6 *oz. grated mild Cheddar*
4 *oz. chopped onion*	*cheese*

Melt bacon fat in a frying pan. Fry meat and half the onion. Heat deep fat for frying. Place tortillas through the deep fat, but do not allow them to brown. Heat the chilli sauce in a pan. Dip tortillas in chilli sauce for 3 minutes. Remove and fill with mixture. Halve and roll into oblong rolls. Place in greased baking dish. Cover with remaining cheese, onions, sauce. Bake in 350 °F oven about 15 minutes, until cheese melts and sauce bubbles. Serves 6 (as part of a mixed plate).

WHITE BREAD
WEST

8 *oz. milk*	½ *pt warm water*
3 *tablespoons sugar*	1 *oz. short shortening*
1 *tablespoon salt*	2 *lb. plain sifted flour*
1 *oz. yeast*	

Scald milk in a saucepan. Pour into a large bowl with sugar and salt. Cool to lukewarm. Add yeast to warm water and let stand 5 minutes. Add to milk mixture. Blend shortening with about ½ the flour into yeast mixture. Beat until smooth with a spoon. Add more flour, a little at a time, until dough cleans the bowl. Turn on to lightly floured cloth-covered board. Knead until dough becomes smooth and little bubbles can be seen beneath the surface. Place in a greased bowl; turn once. Let rise, covered, in a warm draught-free place until doubled in size, about 55 minutes. Punch dough down. Turn over in bowl. Cover and let rise 10 more minutes. Turn out on to board. Divide in two; shape into loaves. Place in greased loaf pans 5 by 9 by 3 inches. Cover. Let rise until doubled in size, about 40 minutes. Bake in a 400°F pre-heated oven until well browned, about 40 minutes. Cool on a rack. Makes 2 loaves.

Sweets

DIVINITY CANDY
MID-ATLANTIC

15 oz. granulated cane sugar $\frac{1}{4}$ teaspoon salt
4 fl. oz. water $\frac{1}{4}$ lb. pecan nuts, chopped
6 oz. light corn syrup   1 teaspoon vanilla
2 egg whites

Boil sugar, water and syrup together until soft-ball stage.
Allow to cool 1 minute while beating egg whites (and salt)
until they are stiff but not dry. Slowly add syrup to egg whites,
beating constantly, until mixture starts to dull and retains its
shape when dropped from a buttered spoon, about 12 minutes.
Quickly add nuts and vanilla. Pour batch on to wax paper
about $\frac{3}{4}$ inch thick. When cold and firm cut into squares.
Makes about 24 pieces.

MAPLE SYRUP FUDGE
NEW ENGLAND

$11\frac{1}{2}$ oz. maple syrup (either   7 oz. granulated sugar
   dark or light)   4 fl. oz. milk

Combine syrup, sugar and milk in a large saucepan. Cook
over low heat to soft-ball stage (235–240 °F). Stir frequently

but avoid stirring the mixture constantly or too vigorously. Remove the pan from the heat and cool mixture to 120 °F. Beat mixture until it is creamy and less glossy. Pour it into a 9 by 9 inch greased pan in about a 1¾-inch layer. Cut the fudge into 1-inch squares when it is nearly cold. If desired, chopped nuts can be added to the fudge before final beating process.

PEANUT BRITTLE
SOUTH

7 oz. salted peanuts	1 oz. butter or margarine
1 teaspoon salt	1 teaspoon baking soda
7 oz. granulated sugar	½ teaspoon vanilla
11½ oz. light corn syrup	2 teaspoons cold water
2 fl. oz. water	

Chop peanuts; sprinkle with salt in a baking tin; warm in oven. Mix sugar, corn syrup and 2 fluid ounces water together in a saucepan. Heat slowly to dissolve sugar. Cook mixture over moderate heat until it reaches 265 °F. Take pan off heat and add butter or margarine. Slowly cook mixture to 290 °F. Mix baking soda, vanilla and cold water together in a cup. Remove pan from heat and stir in baking soda mixture. Stir until mixture rises. Pour into a greased baking pan in a thin sheet over peanuts. When cool enough, spread as thin as possible with fingers. When cold, break into pieces. Makes about 1½ pounds.

PECAN PRALINES
CREOLE

7 oz. brown sugar	½ oz. butter
7 oz. granulated sugar	⅛ teaspoon salt
8 fl. oz. milk	1 tablespoon vanilla extract
4½ oz. chopped pecans	

Combine sugars and milk in a heavy saucepan. Cook the mixture over low heat, stirring constantly until it reaches 224 °F. Add pecans, butter and salt to mixture and cook it until it reaches 234 °F. Remove pan from heat; stir mixture until it becomes slightly granular. Add vanilla extract and pour in buttered pans (tiny individual pans are preferred) or on to a well-oiled baking sheet, then cut before it is hard.

TAFFY APPLES
MIDWEST

4 to 6 firm apples
14 oz. sugar
4 oz. water
⅛ teaspoon cream of tartar

4 oz. butter
1 teaspoon vinegar
4 oz. cream

Wash and dry the apples. Combine the sugar and water in a large saucepan and slowly bring to a boil. Stir until sugar is dissolved. Add cream of tartar, butter, vinegar and cream; cook over medium heat, stirring constantly until mixture reaches 290 °F on sugar thermometer. Remove from heat; dip each apple, on a wooden skewer, into the syrup to coat. Place on a buttered platter to harden. Makes 4 to 6 apples.

Preserves and Pickles

CANTALOUP HONEY
MIDWEST

2 large cantaloups (about
 2½ lb. each)
water
2 lb. sugar

4 fl. oz. lemon juice
½ teaspoon ground nutmeg
¼ teaspoon salt

Cut the cantaloups into wedges; scoop out seeds. Pare and
put flesh through a food mill. Measure resulting pulp and
adjust with water to 2 pints. Combine with sugar, lemon
juice, nutmeg, and salt in a heavy pan. Heat mixture to boiling,
stirring constantly to dissolve the sugar. Cook slowly, until
thick as honey, about an hour and a quarter. Stir mixture
frequently during cooking. Skim and stir for 5 minutes.
Ladle into hot sterilized jars. Seal. Cool completely. Makes
four 8-ounce jars. Serve as a jam.

CIDER APPLE BUTTER
MID-ATLANTIC

12 lb. medium-sized apples
1 gallon sweet cider
2½ lb. sugar

1 tablespoon cinnamon
½ tablespoon cloves

Wash and slice apples. Cook apples with cider until soft. Sieve apples or pass through a food mill; boil the mixture until quite thick, about 1 hour. Add sugar with spices to mixture and boil until thick enough to heap on a spoon. Pack the hot mixture into jars. Process as hot pack.

CORN RELISH
MIDWEST

2 dozen ears corn
½ head white cabbage
4 lb. green tomatoes
6 carrots
6 small onions
2 cucumbers
2 seeded green peppers

4 oz. chopped celery
3 pts vinegar
14 oz. sugar
3½ oz. salt
½ teaspoon dry mustard
½ teaspoon turmeric
⅛ teaspoon cayenne

Cut corn from ears. Chop cabbage, tomatoes, carrots, onions, cucumbers and peppers. Combine all the vegetables and add 1½ pints of the vinegar. Mix and add remaining vinegar. Heat vegetables in a large pan to boiling point; simmer for 40 minutes. Fill 10 sterilized jars with the mixture; seal. Use with cold meat.

BUCK AND BRECK
MID-ATLANTIC

6½ pts cider vinegar
1 lb. brown sugar
6 oz. salt
4 oz. grated horseradish
2 oz. whole cloves
2 oz. black pepper
2 oz. ginger
2 oz. white mustard seed
2 oz. ground mustard seed

2 oz. celery seed
1 oz. turmeric
12 oz. chopped onions
12 oz. chopped celery
12 oz. chopped cabbage
12 oz. chopped tomatoes
12 oz. chopped red peppers
12 oz. chopped green peppers

Put vinegar and seasonings in a 2-gallon crock. Add the vegetables to the mixture until the crock is full. Make sure vinegar covers entire mixture. Mix thoroughly. Cover tightly and let stand for at least three months. Serve as a relish.

PICKLED PEACHES
MID-ATLANTIC

8 2-inch pieces of stick cinnamon	2 lb. sugar
	1½ pts mild cider vinegar
2 tablespoons whole cloves	8 lb. small peaches

Put cinnamon and cloves in muslin bag. Cook with sugar and vinegar for 10 minutes. Peel peaches. Add peaches to vinegar mixture and cook until tender but not broken, about 25 minutes. Let stand overnight. The next day remove spice bag. Drain syrup and boil until thick. Pack peaches in hot sterile jars. Pour hot syrup over peaches, filling jars to top. Seal tightly. Makes 6 pints.

VENISON MINCEMEAT
WEST

2 lb. cooked venison	3 teaspoons allspice
1 lb. beef suet	3 teaspoons cinnamon
6 lb. apples, chopped	3 teaspoons salt
2 lb. currants	2 teaspoons nutmeg
2 lb. seedless raisins	1 teaspoon cloves
1 lb. light raisins	¼ teaspoon ginger
1 lb. candied peel	3 oranges
2½ lb. brown sugar	3¼ pts cider

Chop or grind venison and suet. Mix with chopped apples, currants, raisins and peel. Add sugar, spices, juice of oranges, finely chopped rind of one orange and cider. Simmer in a large heavy saucepan for 30 minutes. Pack hot into jars. Seal and process. Makes enough for twelve 9-inch pies.

WATERMELON PICKLE
SOUTH

5 *lb. watermelon rind*	10 *fl. oz. white vinegar*
6 *pts water*	20 *drops oil of cloves*
6 *lb. sugar*	29 *drops oil of cinnamon*

Cut green and red rind from outer skin into 1-inch pieces. Soak in 3 pints of water overnight. Drain and rinse the rind. Cover with the remaining 3 pints of water in a large saucepan. Bring to a boil; simmer 8 minutes. Drain rind and place in an earthenware crock. Add sugar, vinegar and spices. Allow to stand for 12 hours, stirring frequently. Remove mixture to a saucepan; then cook for 8 minutes. Return mixture to the crock; let stand 5 days, stirring occasionally. Put into sterile jars; seal. Makes about 10 pints.

Index

275

Index

Index

Index

Index

Index

283

Index

rainbow trout, broiled, 82, 150
raisin pie: see funeral pie
raisin-nut bread pudding, 232–3
ramps, 64
rancho sage, 94
raspberry vinegar, 84
rattlesnake, 96
razorback, 64
razor clams, fried, 103
red bean purée, 54, 202
red eye, 94; red eye gravy, 173
red fish, court bouillon, 145–6
red flannel hash, 29, 156, 158
Republican cake, 29
Rhode Island johnny cake, 28, 233
rhubarb: pieplant pie, 75; sherbert, 104, 233; wine, 84
rice: bread, philpy, 46; calas, 51, 254–255; limping Susan, 45; New Orleans, 53; peas, pilau, 46; wild, 85, 207
rinktum ditty, 113
rivel soup, 113
rockfish, stuffed, 37, 147
Rocky Mountain trout, 76
rodeo roast, 85
Roquefort cheese dressing, 218
rosin baked potatoes, 76
rosina boi, 113
rotgut, 94
roux, 54
Russian dressing, 37

saffron, 89
sagebrush honey, 85
salads, 209–14; avocado moulded, 209; bar, 76; bean sauce, 90; cactus, 90, chicken, 70, 186; coleslaw, 210; creamy fruit, 210; dressings, 217–219; dressings, boiled, 24; hot green, 73, 211; hot pea, 73; hot potato, 73; luncheon chef salad bowl, 211; mock chicken, 45–6; moulded pineapple carrot, 213; orange and carrot gelatine, 74, 212; overnight, 74; palmetto, 46; pear, 104; poke, 47, 63; potato, 213;

purslane, 214; Seven-Up, 104; soufflé meat, 212; stuffed prunes, 214; sunshine coleslaw, 209–10; wilted, 78
Sally Lunn, 37, 243–4
salmon: Fourth of July dinner, 26–7; loaf, 147–8; lomi lomi, 105, 107, 148; lox and bagels, 36; sour cream dip, 103, 220
salsa de chile tostado, 94
salt, 108; fish dinner, 29; rising bread, 64
sambogurgers: see craburgers
samp: see pearl hominy
sandwiches: barbecued beef, 152–3; bridge club, 33; burgers, 34; club, 34; Cuban, 44; hobo, 73; Monte Cristo, 103–4; oyster loaf, 53, 136; poor boy, 54, 260; sloppy joes, 77; submarine, 38; western, 104
Saratoga chios, 37
sassafras, 55–6; powder, 52; tea, 94
sauces and dressings, 76, 215–20; adobo, 89; apricot sauce honi, 219; bar-b-cue, 90; barbecue sauce, 177; Béchamel, 23–4; bul kogi barbecue sauce, 215; celery seed, 217; chilli, 220; crab, 34, 102; eye gravy, 64; french, 217–18; fruit butters, 72; guacamole, 220; goupe, 72; gravy, 72; hard sauce, 229; honey-orange, 216; hot stuff, 53; Italian dressing, 218; lemon butter, 219; lobster, 35; milk gravy, 168–9; old sour, 46; Palace Hotel, 104; red eye gravy, 173; Roquefort cheese dressing, 218; Russian, 37; salad, 24, 217–19; salmon sour cream dip, 103, 220; salsa de chile tostado, 94; sauce Arnaud, 55; sauce remoulade creole, 55, 215; shrimp paste, 47; sour cream, 216; sucre brulé, 258–9; tabasco, 55; tartare, 216; thousand island, 39, 217; tomato gravy, 175; veal foot, 30; wine salad, 104, 219
sausage: chorizon, 92; Spanish, 51

285

Index

Index